Christmas 1999

Julian

You probably k
before reading tu
will be no end to,

C000157845

STOCKPORT COUNTY FOOTBALL CLUB: An A-Z

Dean Hayes

Loads of Love.
Vanessa.
xx
x

Published by Sigma Leisure – an imprint of
Sigma Press, 1 South Oak Lane, Wilmslow, Cheshire SK9 6AR, England.

British Library Cataloguing in Publication Data
A CIP record for this book is available from the British Library.

ISBN: 1-85058-641-1

Typesetting and Design by: Sigma Press, Wilmslow, Cheshire.

Printed by: MFP Design & Print

Cover Design: The Agency, Wilmslow

Acknowledgements

Photographs: *Stockport Express Advertiser, Lancashire Evening Post*, Smith Davis Press Agency and the author's personal collection.

Information: Stockport County F.C.; The Association of Football Statisticians: The Football League Ltd: The British Newspaper Library: Stockport Local Studies Library and The Harris Library, Preston. Thanks also to the following individuals: John Gaskin; Cyril Walker junior; Matt Horn; Ben Hayes; Iain Price; Stephen Whittle and Robert Lomas.

Bibliography: *The History of Stockport County AFC* 1883-1965 by Simon Myers; *Stockport County 1883-1983, 100 Years Centenary* edited by Howard Jones and written by Tom Turton. *Stockport County : A Complete Record* by Peter Freeman with Richard Harnwell. The vast collection of programmes, handbooks and scrapbooks of John Gaskin. A selection of local newspapers including *Cheshire Daily Echo, Stockport Chronicle* and *Cheshire County News*. Football League Players' Records; Barclays Club Directories; Rothman's Yearbooks.

A

ABANDONED MATCHES

An abandoned match may be defined as one which is called off by the referee whilst it is in progress because conditions do not permit it to be completed. Far fewer matches are abandoned in modern times because if there is some doubt about the possibility of playing the full game, the match is more likely to be postponed.

On 6th January 1900, the game against Haydock was played in a torrential downpour and after 65 minutes with County leading 5-1, the Haydock players wanted the referee to abandon the game as the pitch was completely waterlogged. When the referee refused, six Haydock players walked off and in the next quarter-of-an-hour, County scored a further four goals before the referee abandoned the game! Below is a full list of abandoned matches involving the Hatters.

Date	Opponents	Venue	Score	Reason
11.04.1896	Rossendale	Away	2-1	Storm (70 minutes)*
06.01.1900	Haydock	Home	9-1	Waterlogged (80 minutes)*
16.11.1901	Crewe	Home	0-0	Fog (45 minutes)
10.01.1903	Gainsborough.T	Away	1-1	Bad Light (86 minutes)
16.11.1904	Glossop	Home	0-0	Fog (100 minutes)
21.11.1904	Glossop	Home	0-0	Snow (45 minutes)
16.01.1909	Grimsby Town	Away	2-0	Bad Light (75 minutes)
11.01.1913	Everton	Away	1-1	Fog (48 minutes)
16.01.1926	Oldham Ath	Away	2-2	Fog (80 minutes)
30.09.1929	Lincoln City	Away	1-1	Bad Light (80 minutes)
20.04 1935	Rotherham United	Away	0-1	Thunderstorm (77 minutes)
22.02.1936	Walsall	Away	0-0	Snow (34 minutes)
12.12.1936	New Brighton	Home	1-1	Fog (77 minutes)
27.12.1937	Newcastle United	Home	2-2	Fog (75 minutes)
26.12.1938	Oldham Ath	Away	1-0	Fog (63 minutes)
13.12.1947	Shrewsbury	Home	1-1	Bad Light (112 minutes)
26.12.1959	Millwall	Away	1-0	Waterlogged (65 minutes)
20.02.1960	Crewe	Home	0-0	Waterlogged (57 minutes)
27.01.1962	Workington	Home	0-0	Fog (37 minutes)
05.12.1964	Grimsby Town	Home	0-0	Fog (50 minutes)
18.02.1977	Bradford City	Home	1-2	Waterlogged (71 minutes)

* Result Stood

AGGREGATE SCORE

Stockport County's highest aggregate score in any competition came in the Football League Cup in September 1996, against Sheffield United. The Hatters won the first leg of this second round tie at Edgeley Park 2-1 before travelling to Bramall Lane and winning 5-2 to give them a 7-3 win on aggregate.

ALLCHURCH, LEN

Len Allchurch followed his brother Ivor by representing Wales Schoolboys and at the age of 14 after playing for Swansea Schoolboys, he joined the Vetch Field ground staff where his older brother was in the first team. He made his debut for the Swans at 17, but it wasn't until he had served two years National Service in the Army that he established himself in the Swansea side. When he was 21, he won the first of 11 Welsh caps when he played against Northern Ireland in Belfast, forming a left-wing partnership with his brother Ivor. He had played in 272 League games for the Vetch Field club when in March 1961, Sheffield United paid £18,000 for his services.

In his first season at Bramall Lane he helped the Blades win promotion to the First Division but in the summer of 1965 after appearing in 123 League games for the Yorkshire club he joined County for £10,000.

He scored on his debut in a 2-1 home defeat by Tranmere Rovers on 6th September 1965, and in 1966-67 played an important role as the club won the Fourth Division championship. The winger continued to display his craft in the Third Division the following season and went on to score 16 goals in 145 first team games before returning to Swansea in September 1969.

He continued to play for the Swans until he was 37 years of age, appearing in 342 League games in his two spells with the club.

ANGELL, BRETT

From being a non-contract player at Portsmouth, the Marlborough-born forward joined Cheltenham Town from where Derby County signed him for £40,000 in February 1988. Though he hadn't made a single first team appearance for the Rams, County manager Asa Hartford paid £33,000 to bring Angell to Edgeley Park. After making his County debut in a 1-1 draw at Scarborough on 22nd October 1988,

Brett Angell

Angell found that he faced stiff competition for a first team forward place from the more experienced Tony Caldwell, Bob Colville and Rodger Wylde.

In 1989-90, Angell was the club's leading scorer with 23 goals in 44 league games including a hat-trick in a 4-2 home win over Scunthorpe United and four goals in a 6-0 defeat of Hartlepool United at Edgeley Park as County finished fourth to win a play-off place.

In the summer of 1990, Angell rather surprisingly opted to leave Stockport and join Southend United who had gained automatic promotion to the Third Division. Despite a number of niggling injuries at Roots Hall, he helped them to win promotion in 1990-91. He had scored 53 goals in 126 League and Cup games before in January 1994, he was transferred to Everton for £500,000.

After just over twelve months at Goodison, he moved to Sunderland for £600,000 but over the next year he had loan spells at Sheffield United and West Bromwich Albion before returning to Edgeley Park for the start of the 1996-97 season. It was a most successful season for Angell, for not only did the club win promotion to the First Division and reach the League Cup semi-finals, but Angell was the club's top scorer with 19 League and Cup goals.

APPEARANCES

Andy Thorpe holds the record for the greatest number of appearances in a Stockport County shirt with a total of 555 games to his credit between 1978 and 1992. Including appearances as a substitute, Thorpe played 489 league games, 14 FA Cup games, 33 League Cup games and 19 games in divisional competitions. The players with the highest number of appearances are:

Player	League	FA Cup	F.Lg. Cup	Others	total
Andy Thorpe	484(5)	14	32(1)	18(1)	548(7)
Bob Murray	465	27	3	0	495
John Rutter	400(2)	16	29	4	449(2)
Bill Bocking	366	24	0	6	396
Trevor Porteous	337	21	6	0	364
Jim Gannon	271(9)	15	27(2)	37(2)	350(13)
Bill McCulloch	309	29	0	0	338
John Price	292(20)	17(1)	15	0	324(21)
Bill Williams	257(3)	12	16	26	311(3)
Chris Beaumont	238(20)	15	14(3)	34(2)	301(25)

ARMSTRONG, ALUN

Blond Geordie striker Alun Armstrong joined Stockport County from Newcastle United for a fee of £50,000 in June 1994. He made a goal-scoring debut in a 4-1 home win over Cardiff City on the opening day of the 1994-95 season and went on to become the club's leading scorer with 15 League and Cup goals. He top scored for the second season running in 1995-96 with 18 League and Cup goals and after scoring against Everton in both FA Cup games, he began to attract a host of Premiership scouts. After two seasons of playing without a regular up-front partner, Brett Angell returned to Edgeley Park for the start of the 1996-97 campaign and Armstrong's play definitely benefited from playing alongside the experienced striker. Though not as prolific as in his first two seasons, a number of his 13 goals were spectacular and important, especially his two in the 5-2 win at Sheffield United.

After having scored 61 goals in 196 first team games for the Hatters, Armstrong left Edgeley Park to return to his native north-east to play for Bryan Robson's Middlesbrough.

ASHWORTH, DAVID

David Ashworth was appointed as Oldham Athletic's first manager, coinciding with the club's return to Boundary Park from Hudson Fold in 1906. A first-class referee from Waterford, he was said to be only about five feet in height and therefore must have been one of the smallest managers ever. Within four years of him taking charge, he had guided the team from the Lancashire Combination to the First Division of the Football League. David Ashworth was usually seen sporting a bowler hat and with a waxed moustache. His rather stern appearance obviously disguised a strong sense of humour, for he was said to wear his 'tash with both ends upturned after a win, both ends down after a defeat and one up and one down after a draw.'

During the close seasons of 1914, he resigned to join Stockport County and though in that 1914-15 season the club could only finish in 14th place, they secured 37 points, their highest total since their entry into the Football League. He continued to be in charge at Edgeley Park throughout the war years but in December 1919, he took charge at Liverpool. After twice finishing in fourth place, he took them to the First Division championship in 1921-22. He was well on course for a second successive League championship with Liverpool when the Oldham directors persuaded him to return to Boundary Park. Sadly, he arrived too late to save the side from its first-ever relegation and after just one season in the Second Division he left for Manchester City, where he stayed for 16 months.

Subsequent appointments included spells as manager at Walsall, Caernarvon and Llanelli before he scouted for Blackpool. Affectionately known as 'Little Dave' he died at Blackpool in March 1947, aged 79 years.

ASSOCIATE MEMBERS CUP

The early rounds of this competition, announced by the Football League in December 1983, were run on knockout lines and played on a regional basis. One of the founder entrants, County were drawn at home to Crewe Alexandra in the first round but lost 3-0 on penalties after the game had finished 2-2 after extra-time.

ATKINS, BILL

Though he was born in Bingley, Yorkshire, Bill Atkins began his career with Swindon Town where he scored 28 goals in 75 league games before returning to his native county to play for Halifax Town. His 34 goals in 78 games for the Shaymen impressed County who signed him in March 1967, in an exchange deal, which took David Shaw-cross to the Yorkshire club.

He played his first game for the Hatters in a 1-0 win against his old club at The Shay and went on to help County win the Fourth Division championship, scoring three goals in the last 14 games of the season.

In 1967-68 Atkins scored 22 goals in 49 League and Cup games including a hat trick in a League Cup first round replay win over Crewe Alexandra. The following season, Atkins was the club's leading scorer with 20 goals despite missing the last nine games of the campaign.

After scoring 45 goals in 102 League and Cup games for County, he joined Portsmouth, but failed to settle on the south coast and returned to play for Halifax, where he completed 200 appearances.

He later played for Rochdale before ending his league career with Darlington.

ATTENDANCES – AVERAGE

Stockport County's average home league attendances over the past ten years have been as follows:

1988-89	2,792
1989-90	3,899
1990-91	3,562
1991-92	4,896
1992-93	5,504
1993-94	5,090
1994-95	4,525
1995-96	5,903
1996-97	6,424
1997-98	8,322

ATTENDANCES – HIGHEST

The record attendance at Edgeley Park is 27,833 for the fifth round FA Cup game with Liverpool on 11th February 1950. Alex Herd scored for County in the dying minutes but earlier goals from Joe Fagan and Albert Stubbins gave the visitors a 2-1 win.

ATTENDANCE – LOWEST

The lowest attendance for a first team fixture at Edgeley Park is 1,000 for the visit of Carlisle United in a Freight Rover Trophy match on 8th December 1986. For the record, the visitors won 1-0.

AUTOGLASS TROPHY

The Autoglass Trophy replaced the Leyland Daf Cup for the 1991-92 season. County made a disastrous start in the competition, losing 4-0

Autoglass Trophy v. Stoke City, 1992

at Carlisle United in front of an attendance of just 894. Thankfully though they were able to progress to the knockout stages of the competition as a result of a Jim Gannon hat trick in a 3-0 home win over York City. The first round proper saw them return to Brunton Park but this time a Kevin Francis hat-trick helped County gain revenge with a 3-1 defeat of the Cumbrian side. In the second round, another Kevin Francis hat trick demolished Hartlepool United who were beaten 3-0. In the Northern Section semi-final, goals from Ward and Wheeler gave County a 2-1 win at Crewe and a place in the two-legged Northern Section final. In the first leg at Turf Moor, a Kevin Francis goal divided the teams and though the second leg at Edgeley Park was

Autoglass Trophy v. Port Vale, 1993

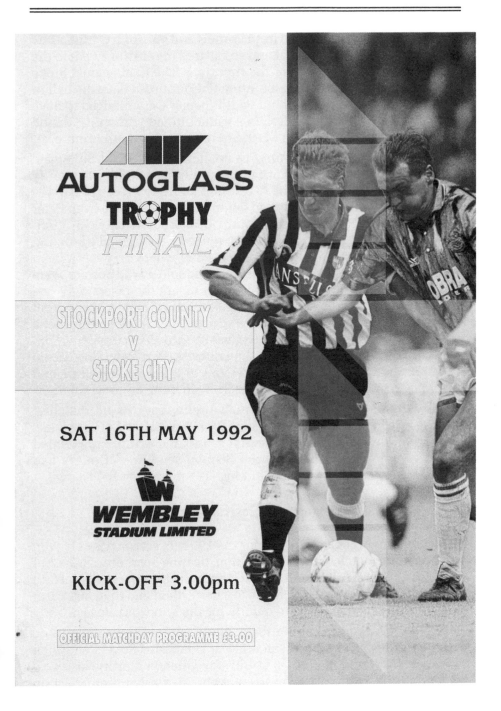

AUTOGLASS
TROPHY
FINAL

STOCKPORT COUNTY
v
STOKE CITY

SAT 16TH MAY 1992

WEMBLEY
STADIUM LIMITED

KICK-OFF 3.00pm

OFFICIAL MATCHDAY PROGRAMME £3.00

hardly a classic, another goal from Francis and one from Gannon saw County home 2-1 on the night and so assured the club of a visit to the Twin Towers of Wembley for the first time. The final against Stoke City was something of a disappointment. County did have the ball in the Stoke net in the first half but Paul Wheeler was adjudged to have fouled Stoke 'keeper Peter Fox. In a game littered with fouls, the tie was won for the Potters by a Mark Stein goal in the 68th minute.

The following season, County beat Chesterfield 3-0 at Saltergate and Chester 2-0 at Edgeley Park in the preliminary round to qualify for the knockout stages. In the first round an Andy Preece strike was enough to beat Hartlepool United before two goals apiece from Peter Ward and Kevin Francis helped County beat Bradford City 4-3 at Valley Parade. In the semi-final, County played Chesterfield again and won 2-1 to reach the Northern Section Final where they met Wigan Athletic. In a one-sided first leg at Springfield Park, County were grateful to a late Jim Gannon goal which meant they were only one goal in arrears for the second leg. In the return match, goals from Ward and Francis gave County a 2-0 win and a visit to Wembley for a second successive year in the Autoglass Trophy. This time, their opponents were another club from the Potteries, Port Vale. Goals from Paul Kerr and Bernie Slaven gave Vale a 2-0 half-time lead and though Kevin Francis pulled one back, Vale hung on to win 2-1.

In 1993-94, County won both their preliminary round matches, beating Wigan Athletic 2-0 at Edgeley Park and Bury 3-1 at Gigg Lane. Rochdale were beaten 4-0 in the first round and Scunthorpe United 2-0 in round two. In the Northern Section semi-final, County had enough chances to win the tie, but lost 1-0 at Huddersfield Town.

AUTOWINDSCREEN SHIELD

Replacing the Autoglass Trophy for the 1994-95 season, County won their opening match in this competition, beating Scarborough 3-1 but then lost 2-1 at Rochdale in the Northern Section quarter-finals. In 1995-96, County drew 1-1 at home to Chesterfield and then lost 1-0 at Notts County and so failed to qualify for the knockout stages.

In 1996-97, the last season that County entered the competition, they won their first round match 2-1 at Doncaster Rovers and then their second round match 1-0 at Burnley where a Martin Nash goal separated the teams. Drawn away again in the Northern Section quarter-final, County won 2-1 at Bury and so faced the prospect of travelling to Gresty Road for a Northern Section semi-final.

In a hard fought contest, the game ended 1-1 after extra-time before County triumphed 5-3 on penalties. In the Northern Section Final first leg, County lost 2-0 at Carlisle United where Owen Archdeacon scored a last minute penalty for the home side. A crowd of 8,593 cheered County on at Edgeley Park in the second leg but the game was goal-less and it was the Cumbrian side that went on to Wembley where they beat Colchester United 4-3 on penalties after a goal-less game.

AWAY MATCHES

County's best away win in the League came in 1965-66 when they won 7-1 at Bradford City with Len White scoring a hat trick. They had scored seven goals in a league match eleven seasons earlier when they beat Chesterfield 7-3 at Saltergate. In 1912-13 they won 7-2 at King's Lynn in the qualifying fifth round of the FA Cup and in 1952-53 beat North Shields 6-2 in the first round proper.

In their Lancashire League days, County beat Heywood Central 9-1 on 29th December 1894.

The club's worst league defeat on away soil came at Chesterfield on 19th April 1902, when the home side thrashed the Hatters 8-1.

County have conceded nine goals in their pre-league days and in wartime matches but the club's heaviest defeat in all matches came on Boxing Day 1942 when they lost 10-0 at Bury in a North Regional League Second Championship match.

AWAY SEASONS

The club's highest number of away wins came in 1929-30 when they won 13 of their 21 matches in finishing runners-up in the Third Division (North).

County have failed to win a single away game in seasons 1912-13 and 1925-26 when they had to re-apply for re-election to the Second Division and were relegated to the Third Division respectively.

B

BAD LUCK!

On 4th October 1913, in a Second Division match between Stockport County and Fulham, Norman Wood the County inside-left headed through his own goal in the 10th minute in attempting to clear a corner kick, to put Fulham ahead. Five minutes later, he accidentally knocked the ball down with his hand in the penalty area and Fulham increased their lead from the resultant spot-kick. Soon afterwards at the other end, Stockport's William Gault was brought down in the penalty area. Wood took the penalty-kick but shot straight at the Fulham 'keeper. Fulham won 3-1.

BEATTIE, ANDY

Andy Beattie joined Preston North End from Scottish non-League side Inverurie Loco for £150 in March 1935, and after impressing on a short tour of Scotland, he made his league debut in the last game of that season at West Bromwich Albion.

A stylish defender noted for his coolness and crisp tackling, he appeared in the 1937 FA Cup Final when North End lost 3-1 to Sunderland but gained a winners' medal the following year when Huddersfield were beaten 1-0 thanks to a last-minute penalty by George Mutch.

He won seven international caps for Scotland before 1939 and was never on the losing side. During the war he turned out for a number of other clubs and represented the FA, British Army and Northern Command. He appeared for Preston in the War Cup Final at Wembley in May 1941, against Arsenal, which the Deepdale club won after a replay.

Turning to football management he became secretary-manager of Barrow in the Third Division (North). After a disagreement with the club's chairman in August 1948, Beattie resigned but this was not accepted by the other directors. As a consequence, the chairman left and Beattie was reinstated.

In March 1949, he moved to Stockport County as manager. In his first full season, County finished in tenth place in the League but equalled their best-ever FA Cup run in reaching the fifth round where they lost to Liverpool. County finished in the same position in 1950-51 but the following season moved up to third place.

In April 1952, he was on the move again, this time to Huddersfield Town. He soon found success, leading the Yorkshire club to promotion to the First Division in his first season. In 1953-54 Huddersfield finished third in the top flight but after they were relegated in 1955-56 Beattie was sacked the following November.

Beattie had before this taken charge of the Scottish national side but resigned in the middle of the 1954 World Cup, claiming lack of support. He was surprisingly given another chance in 1959 but a year later was sacked after preferring to watch a league game than Scotland.

He later managed Carlisle United, Nottingham Forest and had spells as caretaker-manager with Plymouth Argyle and Wolverhampton Wanderers before becoming assistant-manager at Sheffield United. There followed spells as scout for Brentford, Wolves, Walsall, Liverpool and Notts County and when he died in September 1983, he had enjoyed a long and relatively successful career in the game.

Andy Beattie

BEAUMONT, CHRIS

Chris Beaumont was spotted playing amateur football by Denaby United where he played alongside Simon Bergara, Danny Bergara's son. When Bergara senior became manager of Rochdale, he brought Beaumont to Spotland on a three-month trial. However, after only one month he was offered a full-time contract and made a goal-scoring debut as a substitute in a 3-3 Littlewoods Cup draw with Burnley.

During Beaumont's first season at Rochdale, Bergara had left to become manager of Stockport County and in the summer of 1989 he brought the Sheffield-born midfielder to Edgeley Park for a fee of £8,000.

Beaumont scored on his County debut in a 1-1 draw at home to Torquay United on the opening day of the 1989-90 season but was then badly injured and didn't regain his place for another six months.

Able to play in a variety of positions he was most productive supporting the two front players from a wide position on either flank. Beaumont appeared in all of the club's four Wembley appearances and is the only County player to appear in all ten play-off matches for the club. During the 1993-94 play-off final against Burnley, his early goal was marred by his sending-off but Beaumont who is one of foot-

Chris Beaumont

ball's gentlemen put it behind him and went on to score 51 goals in 326 first team games for the club before a fee of £30,000 took him to Chesterfield in the summer of 1996.

Chris Beaumont

BERGARA, DANNY

Born in Uruguay, Danny Bergara played for Racing Club and for his country's Under-21 side before in 1962 he joined Spanish club Real Majorca. After winning a Second Division championship medal with Majorca in 1965 he left to play for Seville where he was the club's top scorer and won another Second Division title.

Eventually he carved out for himself a career in coaching in England. It was Harry Haslam who first employed him as a coach at Luton Town and then as his assistant at Sheffield United.

In 1980 he became the first non-Englishman to take charge of the England Youth team before later coaching in Brunei. In January 1985, he returned to England to take up a coaching position with Middlesbrough but after the receivers were brought in he returned to Bramall Lane, eventually becoming assistant-manager to Billy McEwan. After McEwan's dismissal in January 1988, Bergara found himself as the Blades' caretaker-manager but when Dave Bassett was appointed the new manager, Bergara left to become manager of Rochdale. In his only season at Spotland, he impressed quite a few people and in March 1989, Stockport County appointed him manager.

He made a disappointing start with the side failing to win any of his first 12 games in charge but in

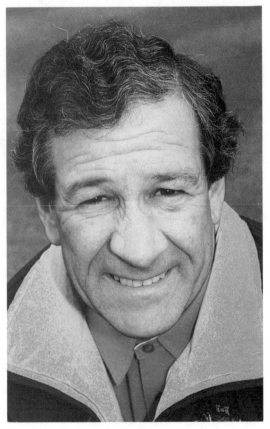

Danny Bergara

1989-90 he took the club to the Fourth Division play-offs where they lost 6-0 on aggregate to Chesterfield. The following season however, they went straight up as runners-up to Darlington after a run of eight wins in their last nine matches. County were unlucky not to be promoted again the following season. After finishing fifth they reached the play-off final at Wembley where they lost 2-1 to Peterborough United.

The week before, they had lost again at Wembley, this time 1-0 to Stoke City in the final of the Autoglass Trophy.

Stockport had another good season under Bergara in 1992-93. They reached the play-offs but lost on aggregate 2-1 to Port Vale. Four days later they met each other again in the final of the Autoglass Trophy at Wembley and County lost again 2-1. They reached the play-offs again in 1993-94 but after having two players sent off, lost 2-1 to Burnley in the Wembley Final.

Sadly in March 1995, after six good years at Edgeley Park, the Uruguayan-born manager was sacked, reportedly after an altercation with chairman Brendan Elwood.

BEST STARTS

County were unbeaten for the first seven games of both the 1929-30 and 1936-37 seasons. In 1929-30 they won five and drew two of their opening fixtures before losing 3-2 at home to Crewe Alexandra and ended the season as runners-up in the Third Division (North). In 1936-37, County won four and drew three of their opening seven matches before losing 3-0 at Port Vale. Losing just five matches, the club won the Third Division (North) championship and were promoted to the Second Division.

BIGGEST DEFEATS

The club's biggest defeat in the Football League occurred on 19th April 1902, when they were hammered 8-1 by Chesterfield at Saltergate. However, it wasn't so surprising as County fielded a side with only seven men. The absent four had missed the train from Stockport and to make matters worse, leading scorer Chesworth broke a rib in the first half. Chesterfield later reported County to the Football League and they were fined £5.

BIGGEST WIN

The club's biggest win is 13-0 over Halifax Town on 6th January 1934. Playing with a strong wind in the first-half, County were only two goals up as half-time arrived but in a second-half in which they played the ball on the ground, they scored another 11 goals, including eight goals in an incredible 16-minute spell!

BLACK, ANDY

Andy Black made a name for himself before the outbreak of the Second World War, having scored 105 goals in 136 league matches for Heart of Midlothian. He was the first player to score a hat trick against Rangers at Ibrox, a performance that led to him winning the first of three full international caps for Scotland when he played against Czechoslovakia. The goal-scoring inside-forward scored on all his three appearances for Scotland but his career at international level suffered because of the hostilities.

During the war, he 'guested' for a number of clubs, one of which was Portsmouth and in a 16-1 win over Clapton Orient, he scored eight of the goals.

In June 1946, he joined Manchester City and in his first season at Maine Road scored 15 goals in 37 games as City won the Second Division championship. In four seasons with the club he scored 52 goals in 146 games but after City's relegation in 1949-50 he moved the short distance to Edgeley Park.

He made his debut for County in the opening game of the 1950-51 season, scoring the first goal in a 3-1 win over Bradford City. He ended the season as the club's top scorer with 17 goals including a hat-trick in a 4-0 Boxing Day win over New Brighton.

In the next two seasons he was supported by the prolific Jack Connor but it didn't stop Black scoring four goals in a 6-0 win over Accrington Stanley in December 1951. By the time he retired at the end of the 1952-53 season, the popular Scot had scored 39 goals in 101 League and Cup games.

BOARDMAN, BEN

Joining Stockport County from Macclesfield in the summer of 1924, Ben Boardman began his Edgeley Park career as understudy to Eddie Critchley. Though he made his debut in a 2-0 home win over Oldham

Athletic in September 1924, it was 1926-27 before he established himself as a regular member of the County side. His best season in terms of goals scored was 1928-29 when he netted 12 in 41 league games. However, Boardman was a brilliant dribbler and passer of the ball and with a remarkable turn of speed, created numerous chances for Joe Smith, Frank Newton and Andy Lincoln.

After scoring 33 goals in 195 League and Cup appearances, Boardman was allowed to leave Edgeley Park and join Manchester City. Sadly, he never played in City's first team, whilst County endured their worst season in the Third Division (North) – a sad end to the League career of one of Stockport County's cleverest players.

BOCKING, BILL

One of County's finest full-backs of all-time, Bill Bocking joined the club in August 1923, having played for Hyde United in the Cheshire League. However, he had to wait more than a year before making his debut at Crystal Palace on 4th October 1924, but then became a permanent fixture in the County side. He captained the Edgeley Park side from 1928 to 1931, but on 30th April 1931, after appearing in 276 games for County he was transferred to Everton.

His transfer led to quite an unusual statistic being created. Bocking's last game for County had been in a 2-2 home draw against Wrexham in the Third Division (North) whilst the following week, the last day of the 1930-31 season, he made his Everton debut against Preston North End in a Second Division fixture. With the Goodison Park club crowned as champions, his next game on the opening day of the 1931-32 campaign was against Birmingham City in the First Division, with the result that within three consecutive league matches, Bocking had played in all three Divisions of the Football League.

In August 1934, after making just 16 League and Cup appearances for the Toffees in three years, he returned to Edgeley Park for a fee of £250.

In his first season back, he captained the club to their best ever FA Cup run as they reached the fifth round before losing to West Bromwich Albion. Two years later, he was an important member of County's Third Division championship-winning side. A player who gave his all to Stockport County, he retired in 1938 after playing in 396 League and Cup games during his two spells with the club.

BOWLES, JACK

Goalkeeper Jack Bowles began his career with his hometown team Cheltenham Town before joining Newport County. After just one season with the Somerton Park club in which he made four appearances, he signed for Accrington Stanley. Again, Bowles only spent one season with the Lancashire club before being transferred to Stockport County in an exchange deal, which took John Daniels and Sammy Hunt to Peel Park.

Nicknamed 'Tiger' he made his debut in a goal-less draw at New Brighton on the opening day of the 1938-39 season and went on to play in 40 games as County finished ninth in the Third Division (North). His performances against the eventual champions, Barnsley made his reputation, especially in the club's 1-0 win at Oakwell on 10th April 1939.

During the war years, Bowles appeared in 34 games for the club and when league football resumed after the hostilities, he was a virtual ever-present, missing just six games in the first four seasons. When County played York City at Bootham Crescent on 15th January 1949; Bowles saved two penalties, a feat he repeated in the same fixture on 25th March 1950.

He played the last of his 306 League and Cup games for County in a 4-2 defeat at Crewe in January 1953, before entering non-League football with Winsford United.

BRADD, LES

Buxton-born Les Bradd had been an apprentice mechanic and apprentice welder before becoming an apprentice footballer with Rotherham United. He only made three first team appearances with the Millmoor club before joining Notts County in October 1967.

During 11 seasons with the Meadow Lane outfit, he played in 398 league games, scoring 125 goals – a club league scoring record.

In August 1978, County boss Mike Summerbee brought Bradd to Edgeley Park. He scored twice on his debut in a 3-0 win over Darlington and at the end of a season in which he formed a deadly striking partnership with Stuart Lee, he had scored 21 goals. These included his only hat-trick for the club in a 4-4 draw at Barnsley. The Oakwell club were leading 4-1 with ten minutes to go when Bradd scored his hat-trick in the space of seven minutes!

As well as playing in his normal position of centre-forward, he played a number of games at centre-half, but in the summer of 1981 after scoring 35 goals in 132 League and Cup games, he signed for Wigan Athletic.

He continued to score freely for the Springfield Park club and notched a hat-trick as the Latics won 7-2 at Scunthorpe United. He had one match on loan for Bristol Rovers before leaving Wigan to play for non-League Kettering in the GM Vauxhall League.

He returned to Notts. County and after a couple of years running their weekly lottery, he became the club's Commercial Manager. In 1994 he crossed the River Trent to take up a similar position with Nottingham Forest.

BROTHERS

Whilst there have been a number of sets of brothers that have played for Stockport County, the most famous are probably the Waterhole brothers. Albert Waterall had played alongside Isaac at Notts County and afters signing for Stockport in 1913, formed a left-wing partnership with brother Tommy. Tommy Waterall made 87 wartime appearances for County, whilst Albert, who played for County for 13 consecutive seasons, including wartime football, appeared in 379 games for the club.

BURGESS, HARRY

After joining the club as an amateur from Nantwich Ramblers, he made his debut in a 4-0 defeat at Hull City in March 1926, but after signing professional forms the following summer, his career blossomed. In 1926-27, Burgess was the club's top scorer with 28 goals in 35 league games including hat-tricks against Wigan Borough (Home 4-1) and Wrexham (Home 3-2) and all four goals in a 4-1 home win over Nelson. Following the arrival of former Bolton star, Joe Smith, who netted 38 goals in 40 games, Burgess turned goal-maker rather than goal-scorer but in 1928-29 he once more found his scoring boots, netting 31 goals in 42 league games including hat-tricks against South Shields (Home 7-1) and Ashington (Home 4-0).

At the end of that season he joined Sheffield Wednesday and after scoring on his debut in a 3-1 win at Aston Villa, ended the season with 19 goals in 39 games as Wednesday won the League Championship. In 1930-31 he netted a hat-trick in a 4-0 win at Blackpool and won the first of four England caps against Northern Ireland. In 1933-34 he top scored for Wednesday, yet surprisingly in March 1935, after scoring 77 goals in 224 games, he was sold to Chelsea.

BURNLEY

On 26th January 1991, County and Burnley met for the eleventh time in League and Cup games in exactly 17 months. The breakdown of first-class matches was: 4 Division Four; 3 Leyland Daf; 2 FA Cup and 2 Rumbelows Cup games.

Between 8th January and 26th January 1991, they met three times, the last two encounters within four days when the Clarets won successive games 3-2 in the Leyland Daf and Fourth Division. Burnley won four games, Stockport three and there were four draws.

BUTLER, JOE

After making his County debut in a 3-2 defeat at Burton Swifts in September 1900, goalkeeper Joe Butler had to wait until 1901-02, the club's second season in the Football League before winning a regular place.

Very highly regarded, Butler was ever-present during the 1903-04 season when the club failed to gain re-election to the Football League. However, despite the interest of a number of top clubs, he stayed at Edgeley Park and in 1904-05 helped County win the Lancashire Combination. In the penultimate game of the season, a 6-0 home win over St Helens Town, Butler celebrated the club's success by slotting home a penalty.

In the summer of 1905, despite the club's successful application to the Second Division, Butler moved to Clapton Orient but after just 24 first team games, he returned to Stockport where he stayed for another two years, taking his total number of League and Cup appearances to 190.

He then joined Glossop where he made 152 consecutive league appearances before being suspended following an incident in a game against Chelsea. On his return from suspension, he joined Sunderland and in 1912-13 won a League Championship medal and a FA Cup runners-up medal.

He later joined Lincoln City but in October 1916, he returned to Edgeley Park to make 37 wartime appearances for County.

CAPACITY

The total capacity of Edgeley Park in 1997-98 was 12,086.

CAPTAINS

Among the many players who have captained the club are left-back **Arthur Layton** who led the club to their first Football League honours when they won the Third Division (North) championship in 1921-22. Bill Bocking who played in 396 League and Cup games for County skippered the club from 1928 to 1931 when they finished runners-up in the Third Division (North) for two consecutive seasons.

Though he only spent two seasons at Edgeley Park, **Percy Downes** was made captain and in 1933-34 he led them to third place in the Third Division (North) as the club scored 115 league goals, 13 of them against Halifax Town.

Goalkeeper **Frank McDonough** captained County to the Third Division (North) championship in 1936-37 but twelve months later, he was released!

In 1992, **David Frain** led County out at Wembley twice in the space of eight days, only for the club to lose 1-0 to Stoke City in the Autoglass Trophy and 2-1 to Peterborough United in the Third Division play-off final.

In 1996-97, **Mike Flynn** captained County to promotion to the First Division and to the semi-finals of the League Cup.

CATTERICK, HARRY

Though he never played League or Cup football for Stockport County, his record for 'guesting' for the club warrants his inclusion. Catterick's father had been both a player and a trainer at Edgeley Park and in fact, managed the club for a short while during the Second World War.

Harry Catterick junior played in every wartime season for County, scoring 98 goals in only 122 appearances including eight hat-Tricks and all four goals in a 4-1 home win over Manchester City in 1944-45.

When the war was over, Catterick played for Everton, scoring 24 goals in 71 League and Cup games before ending his playing career with Crewe Alexandra.

After managing Crewe, Rochdale and Sheffield Wednesday, Catterick took charge at Everton in 1961 and guided the Goodison club to the FA Cup in 1966 and to two League Championships. Following a heart attack in 1972, he was moved sideways into a senior executive role. Sadly, Catterick died at Goodison Park after a FA Cup quarter-final match against Ipswich Town in March 1985. The man who restored pride to the Merseyside club was never afraid to back his own judgement and put his reputation on the line.

CENTURIES

There are only two instances of individual players having scored 100 or more league goals for Stockport County. Jack Connor is the greatest goal-scorer with 132 strikes in his Edgeley Park career(1951-1956) whilst the other centurion is Alf Lythgoe with 104 goals.

Bob Murray holds the club record for the most consecutive League appearances – 213. Other players to have made over 100 consecutive League appearances during their County careers are Harry Hardy (170); Billy Haydock (140); Mike Flynn (133); John Rutter (118); Mike Salmon (118) and Graham Ricketts (115).

CHAIRMEN

Stockport County's longest serving chairman was Ernest Barlow who was elected as the club's chairman on 29th August 1923, and remained in office until his death on 4th September 1954.

CHAMPIONSHIPS

Stockport County have won a divisional championship of the Football League on three occasions.

They won the Third Division (North) championship in 1921-22, opening the campaign with six games without defeat and without conceding a solitary goal. After Grimsby Town had done the 'double' against them, County went on a run of 19 matches with only one defeat and were undefeated from New Year's Day until Good Friday. The next day, County won the Championship when they won 1-0 at Darlington, their nearest rivals. Goalkeeper Harry Hardy was the only ever-present and he kept a record 23 clean sheets.

County won the Third Division (North) championship for a second time in 1936-37. Once again the season began in style as the club embarked on a seven-match unbeaten run. The side's mainstay to success was consistency with the club only losing five of its 42 matches. The Championship wasn't clinched until the final Saturday of the season at Edgeley Park when a record attendance of 26,135 saw County beat Lincoln City 2-0. The club's captain was full-back Bill Bocking but injury prevented him from celebrating County's success on the pitch.

The club last won a divisional championship in 1966-67 when they won the Fourth Division title. After drawing 1-1 in the opening game of the season at Barrow, County won their next five matches and maintained this type of form all the way through the season. The Fourth Division trophy was presented to the club at Edgeley Park before the final match of the season against bottom club Lincoln City. The Sincil Bank club had provided the opposition on the last day of the season in each of County's three championship winning seasons. On this occasion they triumphed 5-4 but could not stop the celebrations that followed.

CHAPMAN, LES

As a player, occupying a midfield position, Les Chapman played in turn for Oldham Athletic, Huddersfield Town, Oldham (again), Stockport County, Bradford City, Rochdale, Stockport (for a second spell) and finally Preston North End. He made over 700 appearances in 22 seasons and appeared in all four divisions of the Football League, plus the NASL with San Jose Earthquakes.

He first joined County at the end of the 1978-79 season and after making his debut in a 2-1 defeat at Walsall on the opening day of the 1979-80 season, he went on to become one of the club's most popular players. However, in February 1980, after making 37 appearances he left Edgeley Park.

Chapman returned to the club in the summer of 1985 but within weeks found himself appointed player-manager after Murphy's departure to Saudi Arabia. When he took charge, County were lying 19th in the Fourth Division and though they lost six of their last eight games, they still finished 11th, their highest position for 17 years. Remarkably, Chapman was sacked before the start of the 1986-87 season and moved to Preston North End as player/assistant-manager. He was appointed team manager at Deepdale in February 1990, succeeding John McGrath. He steered the club away from relegation but as the club con-

Les Chapman

tinued to struggle at the wrong end of Division Three, the director's patience eventually ran out and in September 1992, Chapman was sacked.

CHAPMAN, ROY

He began his playing career with Aston Villa but with first team opportunities limited, he moved to Lincoln City in November 1957, for the first of two spells with the Imps. In August 1961, Raich Carter then manager of Mansfield Town paid £7,000 to take Chapman to Field Mill. There he formed a formidable striking partnership with Ken Wagstaff and in his second season, he helped the club win promotion from the Fourth Division. He had scored 78 goals in 136 league games when in January 1965, he returned to Sincil Bank as player-manager. He later played for Port Vale where he scored 38 times in 77 appearances and Chester before taking over the manager's job at Stafford Rangers.

He had six successful seasons with Stafford, winning the Northern Premier League championship and the FA Trophy in 1972 and taking the club into the fourth round of the FA Cup for the first time in their history. During that run they beat County after a replay!

He became County's manager in September 1975, despite efforts to keep him in the Midlands. Though he was only in charge for a short while, he did bring George Best to the club, the Northern Ireland international turning out for County on three occasions. At the end of the 1975-76 season, the club had to apply for re-election for the third time in five years and Chapman was sacked.

He then returned to non-League management with Stafford Rangers but at the age of only 49 he died whilst playing in a practice game of football at a local sports centre near his home in Stoke.

CLEAN SHEET

This is the colloquial expression to describe a goalkeeper's performance when he does not concede a goal. Harry Hardy in 1921-22 had 23 clean sheets from 38 league appearances as County won the Third Division (North) championship. The best performance in recent years was by Paul Jones in 1996-97 when he kept 18 clean sheets in 46 appearances, plus another four in Cup matches.

CLEMPSON, FRANK

Salford-born Frank Clempson began his league career with Manchester United but in five seasons at Old Trafford, he was restricted to just 15 league appearances in which he scored twice. Eight of these came towards the end of the 1951-52 season when United won the First Division championship.

When he joined County in February 1953, Clempson was an inside-forward but manager Dick Duckworth successfully converted him into a left-half and he became the club's regular penalty-taker.

Clempson gave the club seven years loyal service, scoring 37 goals in 261 League and Cup appearances and in 1954-55 was selected for the Third Division (North) representative side against the Third Division (South).

In 1959 he was transferred to Chester where he was immediately appointed captain but in 1960-61 even his influence couldn't prevent the then Sealand Road club's slide to the bottom of the Fourth Division.

COCKER, LES

Though he had played football for Stockport Boys, Les Cocker had no intention of making a professional career out of the game and had become a painter and decorator before joining the army in 1942. Whilst on leave he went to watch the Hatters play Accrington Stanley in a Western region match. County found themselves a man short and so Cocker stepped in and played at left-half.

It was the beginning of an eight-year association with the Edgeley Park club, with the versatile Cocker making his league debut in a 3-2 defeat at York City in November 1946. He went on to play in 189 League and Cup games and scored 48 goals, three of which helped County to the fifth round of the FA Cup in 1949-50.

He left Stockport in August 1953, and joined Accrington Stanley and in the Peel Park club's best-ever spell he scored 49 goals in 132 League and Cup games.

After hanging up his boots, he became assistant trainer at Accrington and then at Luton before becoming trainer at Leeds United. Forming a good partnership with Don Revie, he had spells as England coach before becoming manager of Doncaster Rovers. Sadly, it was whilst with the Belle Vue club that he collapsed and died during a training session.

COLOURS

Stockport County's present colours are royal blue shirts, white shorts and blue stockings, with their change colours being black and white quartered shirts, black and white halved shorts and black stockings.

When County first joined the Football League in 1900 they wore red jerseys and did so until August 1914, when they began to wear blue and white stripes. During the early 1930s, County changed their colours from blue and white to white and black. This was the idea of the then county manager Fred Westgarth and indeed, the Hatters remained in these colours until the end of the 1964-65 season. The idea of changing to blue for the start of the following season was chairman Vic Bernard's idea of giving the club a completely new image. It seemed to work for in 1966-67 whilst wearing royal blue, County stormed away with the Fourth Division championship.

Surprisingly the very next season saw the club's 'lucky' blue shirts discarded for white with a blue chest band. There then followed all combinations of royal blue and white shirts and even a black and white one, when Mike Summerbee's Argentina shirts were discarded because of the Falklands War.

It wasn't really until the introduction of the popular blue shirts with red flecks in 1991 that County again wore predominantly blue shirts.

COMBINATION

County played their first league match in the Combination on 5th September 1891, but the Green Lane club crowd were disappointed as the visitors Macclesfield won 3-0. In fact, County lost their first six matches before gaining their first success in the competition, a 2-0 win over Chirk on 17th October. At the end of their first season in the Combination, County finished second from the bottom of the League – ten points clear of bottom club Denton.

In 1892-93, County improved to finish sixth in the League before the following season, which was their last in the Combination, they moved up to fourth, only one point behind runners-up Stoke Swifts. Also that season, County beat the champions Everton Reserves 4-0 at Green Lane to inflict upon the Merseyside club their only defeat of the season.

CONNOR, JACK

Jack Connor broke all the club's goal-scoring records during his stay at Edgeley Park and but for the Second World War would have netted an even more impressive record.

It is highly likely that Connor would have started his professional career with Rochdale had it not been for the outbreak of hostilities in 1939 and so throughout the war years, he had to be content with 'guesting' for Gateshead, Darlington, Newcastle United, Carlisle United, Crystal Palace and Ipswich Town.

At the end of the war, he signed for Ipswich Town but after scoring four goals in 12 games, he left to play for Carlisle United, where he had made his home. Two injury-hit seasons saw him net 12 goals in 39 games for the Brunton Park club. Following a loan spell with Ards he eventually joined Rochdale, where his career took off. In 88 league appearances for the Spotland club he scored 42 goals before being signed by Bradford City.

In October 1951, Jack Connor and his wife were in a Bradford cinema when a message was flashed onto the screen, 'Would Jack Connor, Bradford City's centre-forward please go to the foyer'. He was met by County manager Andy Beattie and chairman Ernest Barlow and signed there and then for £2,500. He made his debut the following day in a 0-0 draw at home to Oldham Athletic.

His five seasons at Edgeley Park saw him score two goals every three games. He scored 11 hat-tricks – two of them in consecutive matches in 1953-54 – Crewe Alexandra (Away 5-1) and Chester (home 5-0). He scored four goals in a match twice against Bradford Park Avenue (1954-55 Home 6-0) and Tranmere Rovers (1955-56 Home 7-0) and equalled the club record of five in a game twice, against Workington (1952-53 Home 6-0) and Carlisle United (1955-56 Home 8-1). He was County's top scorer in each of his five seasons with the club and in 217 appearances scored 140 League and Cup goals.

In 1955 he was chosen to represent the Northern Section of the Third Division against the Southern Section and scored in a 2-1 win.

In September 1956, following a dispute with County manager Willie Moir, Connor left Edgeley Park to sign for Crewe Alexandra. He later had a season with non-League Runcorn before hanging up his boots in 1958. He later worked at County as the Pools promoter but after six years took on the same role at Rochdale. He returned to Stockport in 1970, working in the same capacity until 1978.

CONSECUTIVE HOME GAMES

Stockport County played an intense sequence of six home games in succession in 38 days (17th January-24th February 1986). They won three – Preston North End (2-1); Crewe Alexandra (3-0); and Northampton Town (1-0) – drew two – Colchester United (1-1) and Exeter City (1-1) and lost one, Swindon Town (0-2).

CONSECUTIVE SCORING – LONGEST SEQUENCE

Andy Lincoln holds the club record for consecutive scoring when he was on target in nine consecutive League games. His first came in a 2-1 win at Nelson on 25th January 1930, and ended with two goals in a 6-1 home win over Rotherham United on 8th March 1930.

COYLE, TONY

One of the club's most versatile players, he joined County from Albion Rovers in December 1979, for a then record fee of £25,000. Glasgow-born Coyle had played football from a very early age but ensured that he completed his apprenticeship at the Govan shipyards. After trials with Aberdeen, Dundee United, Morton and St Mirren, he opted to play for Second Division Albion Rovers, albeit on a part-time basis.

County boss Jimmy McGuigan had almost signed Coyle when he was in charge at Rotherham United, but had left Millmoor before he could do so.

Following his arrival at Edgeley Park, Coyle who could play both outside-left and on the left side of midfield, went on to be a first team regular for the next seven seasons. He had scored 30 goals in 240 League and Cup games for the Hatters when he was allowed to join Chesterfield in the summer of 1986. Despite playing in an unaccustomed left-back role for the Spireites, he was voted Chesterfield's 'Player of the Year' in his first season at Saltergate. He was released at the end of the 1987-88 season but when a proposed move to Notts. County fell through, he phoned Asa Hartford to ask if he could train with his old club to keep fit.

Injuries then opened the door for Coyle to sign for the club on a week to week contract and in his first game of his second spell he scored in a 4-1 win at Darlington on the opening day of the 1988-89 season. He went on to score three goals in a further 29 appearances for the club before leaving to play for Northwich Victoria. Apart from a month's loan at Exeter City he spent two seasons with the Vics before seeing out his career with Hyde United.

CRICKETERS

The only Stockport County players who were cricketers of real note were Fred Ridgeway, Ken Grieves and Chris Marples.

Fred Ridgeway was an inside-forward who scored three goals in 21 wartime appearances for his home-town club. He played first-class cricket for Kent and took 955 wickets at 23.81 each with a best of eight for 39 against Gloucestershire. He played five Tests for England on the 1951-52 tour of India, two years after his most successful season on the county circuit when he took 105 wickets at 23.32 runs each.

Goalkeeper Ken Grieves played in 43 League and Cup games for County during the 1957-58 season. The Australian-born all-rounder played in 452 first-class matches for Lancashire from 1949 to 1964, scoring 20,802 runs at 33.39 and capturing 235 wickets at 28.80 each.

Goalkeeper Chris Marples was a wicket-keeper/batsman for Derbyshire. He appeared in 26 matches for the County, helping to dismiss 59 batsmen (54 caught, 5 stumped) and made his highest score of 57 against Lancashire at Liverpool in 1986.

CRITCHLEY, EDDIE

Eddie Critchley was discovered playing in junior football in his native Stockport and signed amateur forms for County in September 1921. However, he had to wait over 12 months before making his first team debut in a 2-0 home defeat by Port Vale. Then it was back to the Reserves until his next opportunity to pull on a first team shirt five months later. It was the last match of the season against Southampton at Edgeley Park. County had to win to stay in the Second Division, anything less and they would be making a quick return to the Third Division (North). He didn't let the Hatters down, creating both of Wilf Woodcock's goals in a 3-0 win.

As the flying winger became a first team regular in the County side, a number of top flight clubs showed an interest in signing him. Therefore, it was not surprising when he joined Everton on 22nd December 1926, for a fee of £3,000.

Within three days of his transfer, he made his debut in front of a Christmas Day crowd of 37,500, creating four goals for Dixie Dean in a 5-4 win over Sunderland. He was a key member of Everton's 1927-28 League Championship-winning side and was instrumental in helping Dixie Dean set his unsurpassable record of 60 League goals in one season. Two years later he suffered the trauma of relegation but the Blues bounced back immediately as they won the Second Division title, with Critchley scoring 15 goals. Twelve months later, the First Division championship trophy was once again on display in the Goodison trophy cabinet. He scored 42 goals in 229 games for the Blues before leaving to join Preston North End in 1934. He made 11 appearances for the Deepdale club before ending his career with Port Vale.

CROWD TROUBLE

However unwelcome, crowd disturbances are far from being a modern phenomenon at Football League matches. Sad to relate, there have been a few instances of Edgeley Park having to be closed through disciplinary reasons. One such occasion was because of an incident that happened during County's 3-1 home defeat by Blackpool on 7th January 1911. During the match, the referee Mr Garner of Barnsley was struck by a stone thrown from the crowd and as a result, the ground was closed for two weeks from the end of that month.

D

DAVOCK, MIKE

Though he made his first team debut in a 2-0 defeat at Derby County in April 1957, it was to be another three seasons before the St Helens-born winger won a regular place in the Hatters' side. In 1959-60, Davock was the club's leading scorer with 13 League and Cup goals and though he continued for the next five seasons to score his share of goals, it was as a provider that he is best remembered at Edgeley Park.

Sadly during Davock's time with the club, County were going through one of their worst spells, but the industrious winger remained committed to his one and only Football League club and scored 46 goals in 252 League and Cup appearances before hanging up his boots.

DEBUTS

County's youngest debutante is Steve Massey who was 16 years 337 days old when he came on as a substitute and scored the winning goal in the club's 2-1 home win over Darlington on 28th February 1975.

Both Joe Griffiths (York City Home 3-2 in 1931-32) and Len Barker (Crewe Alexandra Away 3-3 in 1948-49) scored hat-tricks on their County debut, whilst Andy Lincoln (Barrow Home 5-0 in 1929-30) and Joe Hill (Halifax Town Home 13-0 in 1933-34) both scored hat-tricks on their home debut.

DEFEATS – FEWEST

During the 1936-37 season, County went through the 42-match programme and only suffered five defeats as they won the Third Division (North) championship.

DEFEATS – MOST

Stockport's total of 29 defeats during the 1964-65 and 1969-70 seasons are the worst in the club's history. On the first occasion, County finished bottom of the Fourth Division and on the second, they finished bottom of the Third Division and were relegated.

DEFEATS - WORST

County's record defeat was when Chesterfield beat them 8-1 at the Recreation Ground, Saltergate on 19th April 1902. Four players missed the train to Chesterfield and County took to the field with only seven players, three of whom were forwards. During the first-half, County's Frank Chesworth broke his ribs with the result that the Hatters played for the majority of the match with only six players! To make matters worse, Chesterfield reported Stockport to the Football League for playing only seven men and claimed £20 for loss of gate receipts. Though the matter was considered, it was dismissed with County just being fined £5 for turning out a depleted side.

County also conceded eight goals on 4th October 1958, when they lost 8-2 at Colchester United.

The club have lost nine League and Cup matches by a 7-0 score line – Burton United (Division Two 1903-04); Bristol City (Division Two 1905-06); Fulham (Division Two 1912-13); Portsmouth (FA Cup 1948-49); Port Vale (Division Three(North) 1953-54); Aldershot (Division Four 1963-64); Crystal Palace (League Cup 1979-80); Hull City (Division Four 1982-83) and Sheffield Wednesday (League Cup 1986-87).

DEFENSIVE RECORDS

Stockport County's best defensive record was established in 1921-22 and helped the club win the Third Division (North) championship. They conceded just 21 goals in that campaign and were beaten in only six matches.

County's worst defensive record was in 1925-26 when they let in 97 goals to finish bottom of the Second Division.

DISMISSALS

Tommy Charlton enjoyed four successful seasons at Edgeley Park and had scored 29 goals in 99 League and Cup games when he was sent-off in the 2-2 draw at Glossop in February 1913. Whilst serving a three-week suspension for his misdemeanour, he was transferred to Burnley for a fee of £650.

Gene Wilson was another of the club's diminutive wingers and he received his marching orders in an 'A' team fixture against Manchester City. Sent off for arguing, the County player refused to leave the field and was told by the referee that he had ten seconds to get off the pitch, otherwise he would abandon the game. Wilson prolonged his departure sufficiently for the referee to carry out his threat, the game being abandoned.

In the 1994 Second Division play-off final against Burnley at Wembley, County had two players sent-off with Mike Wallace and Chris Beaumont being the culprits.

DOWNES, PERCY

Outside-left Percy Downes began his career with Gainsborough Trinity before joining Blackpool in 1925. When the Seasiders won the Second Division championship in 1929-30, Downes provided the crosses for Jimmy Hampson to score the majority of his 45 goals as well as netting 13 himself. After scoring 33 goals in 158 League and Cup games he left Bloomfield Road and joined Hull City. After just one season he was not retained and moved to Stockport County on a free transfer.

He played his first game for the club at home to Darlington on the opening day of the 1932-33 season, scoring a goal in a 5-1 win. He went on to score 11 goals in 41 games as County finished third in the Third Division (North). He was made club captain before the start of the 1933-34 season and in the 13-0 rout of Halifax Town, he scored four of the goals. Though he only stayed at Edgeley Park for two seasons, he had scored 27 goals in 90 games when he joined Burnley in May 1934. After two seasons at Turf Moor he joined his last league club, Oldham Athletic before returning to see out his career with his first club, Gainsborough Trinity.

DOYLE, BRIAN

Full-back Brian Doyle began his league career with Stoke City for whom he made 17 League appearances before joining Exeter City in April 1954. He played in 104 League games for the Grecians before moving to Second Division Bristol Rovers where he ended his playing career.

After a short spell as coach to Carlisle United, he was appointed manager of Workington but left after just one season in charge. Following another coaching spell with Blackpool, he was appointed manager of Stockport County in March 1972, three months after the departure of Matt Woods. He could do little about County finishing next to the bottom of the Fourth Division and having to apply for re-election but in 1972-73 led them to 13th and into the fourth round of the League Cup after victories over First Division sides Crystal Palace and West Ham United. In 1973-74, County had yet another disastrous season, finishing bottom of the Fourth Division. As the club applied for re-election for the second time in three years with Doyle at the helm, he was sacked.

DRAKE, RAY

Despite being struck down by Meningitis when three years of age, an illness which left him totally deaf in one ear and with only 30% hearing in the other, Ray Drake went on to score an amazing 234 goals from 201 matches for Stockport County, the team he had supported as a boy.

After playing for the Co-op works team, he joined Bramhall in the Lancashire and Cheshire League and in 1953 attended Edgeley Park for a trial. After scoring two goals in the trial match he was signed as a semi-professional. He then spent the next three seasons serving his apprenticeship with County's Reserve side. In 1954-55 he scored 69 goals from 46 matches and the following season added 59 goals from 41 matches. This included all eight goals in an 8-1 win over Cheadle Rovers on Boxing Day 1955.

His chance for first team football finally came on 1st December 1956, when he scored one of the goals in a 3-2 win over Derby County. Drake was on the score sheet in his first four games and scored seven goals in his first six outings. The total included what is believed to be the fastest goal ever scored by a County player when Drake found the net after just 7 seconds of the Christmas Day victory over Accrington Stanley.

On 16th February 1957, Drake scored a hat-trick in a 5-1 win at

Gateshead and a week later scored all four goals in a 4-0 home win over Wrexham. Following these displays there were strong rumours that Drake was going to move to Bolton Wanderers in exchange for England international centre-forward Nat Lofthouse but these didn't materialise.

Following a disagreement with County manager Willie Moir, Drake was transfer listed at £1,000, having scored 19 goals in 23 first team games. Preferring to stay in the north-west he then played non-League football for Altrincham, Hyde United and Cheadle Rovers before hanging up his boots.

DRAWS

Stockport County played their greatest number of drawn league matches in a single season in 1988-89 when 21 of their matches ended all-square and their fewest in 1946-47 when only two of their 42 matches were drawn. The club's highest scoring draw in the league is 4-4, a score line in seven games – Hull City (Away 1931-32); Hull City (Away 1938-39); Crewe Alexandra (Away 1954-55); Gateshead (Away 1954-55); Newport County (Home 1971-72); Swansea City (Away 1976-77); and Barnsley (Away 1978-79).

During the Second World War, County drew 6-6 against Manchester City at Maine Road.

DUCKWORTH, DICK

Dick Duckworth had an exceptionally long career as a player, manager and scout, serving more than a dozen Football League clubs. His playing career was mainly confined to Division Three (North) although he helped Chesterfield to promotion and captained York City when they 'giant-killed' two First Division teams to reach the sixth round of the 1938 FA Cup competition.

York City was Duckworth's first managerial job in the Football League. He had been there just over two years when he was offered a similar post at Stockport County. The York directors agreed to release him from his contract but only on the proviso that he didn't begin his new duties until after the visit of Stockport County on 18th October 1952, a match which York won 3-0.

He soon learned that his new job would be a challenge, as County midway in the league table had just lost leading scorer Alf Lythgoe, who had followed Andy Beattie to Huddersfield Town. Lythgoe claimed that County were not a happy family and that the new manager would have tough job off the field. Twenty-seven Stockport players refuted this claim by signing an open letter. Duckworth never achieved promotion for County in his four years with the club and in May 1956, left to become chief scout at Sheffield United. He later returned to management with Darlington before taking charge at Scunthorpe United.

E

EARLY GROUNDS

Stockport County started life in 1883 as Heaton Norris Rovers and first played at the Heaton Norris Recreation Ground. Within a year, they had moved to Heaton Norris Wanderers cricket ground before in 1885 amalgamating with rivals Heaton Norris and switching to Chorlton's Farm off Didsbury Road. The club moved again in season 1886-87 when they played at the Ash Inn Ground on Manchester Road and soon after moved to Wilkes Field in Belmont Street. In 1889 the club settled at their first enclosed ground at the Nursery Inn, Green Lane.

It was here that the club changed its name to Stockport County and where the players built a stand that had no roof but housed 4,000 spectators. Green Lane was the club's home for 13 years and was where County kicked off their Football League carer before moving to Edgeley Park in 1902.

EDGELEY PARK

When County arrived at Edgeley Park in 1902, they had to share the ground with the rugby team who had played there since 1891. However, within twelve months, the rugby club had folded leaving County as the ground's sole tenants.

County's first Football League match at the ground saw them draw 1-1 with Gainsborough Trinity on 13th September 1902.

In the summer of 1903, a roof was erected at the rear of the Popular side and in 1913 a new Main Stand was built on the Hardcastle Road side of the ground. Two years later, a wooden cover was built at the Cheadle End.

On 23rd July 1935, a fire broke out and completely gutted the Main Stand whilst 12 houses and an adjoining print works were badly damaged in what was described as the biggest blaze seen in Stockport for many years. All the club's records were lost, including fixture lists of the original Heaton Norris Rovers. A series of marquees were erected where the old stand had stood so that players and referee could change and it was most unusual to see County's directors having to stand behind the Cheadle Stand goal instead of sitting in their usual seats.

A year after the fire, a replacement 2,000 seat Main Stand was built at a cost of £7,000 and opened on 24th October 1936, by the League President, Charles Sutcliffe.

On 11th February 1950, Edgeley Park housed its record gate when

Edgeley Park

27,833 witnessed County's FA Cup fifth round tie against Liverpool, which the Reds won 2-1.

In 1956, a sloping roof was added to the Popular Side, whilst the terracing was dedicated to the club's late chairman, Ernest Barlow. Also that year, floodlights were erected at Edgeley Park and first used on 16th October, for the visit of Dutch side Fortuna 54 Geleen.

In 1964, with the club struggling, an offer of help came from the Corporation who bought Edgeley Park for £24,500 and then leased it back at a cost of £900 per year. In the end, the ground did return to County's ownership and as gates fell below the 3,000 mark in 1978, the rear of the Barlow Stand was fenced off and a five-a-side pitch laid.

In 1985, Edgeley Park became designated under the Safety of Sports Grounds Act. The club had just sought re-election and were facing a winding up order. The safety inspectors immediately ordered the demolition of the Cheadle End Stand and for the next ten years, a strip of flat ground lay behind the goal! Also this year, the open Railway End of the ground was reduced to a third of its original height. In all, the club had to spend £150,000 on ground improvements, yet the capacity was still cut to 6,000 including 1,840 seats. The club did consider leaving Edgeley Park but hung on for a further three years until County chairman Brendan Elwood rescued them from the bailiffs again! The chairman's initial aim was to relocate, possibly joining with the council in developing a stadium at Hazel Grove but in the end, the club decided to stay at Edgeley Park.

County supporters were none too upset, especially as promotion in 1991 was sandwiched by four trips to Wembley, before in 1997, the club won promotion again, this time to the First Division.

EDWARDS, NEIL

Goalkeeper Neil Edwards who has been capped by Wales at Schoolboy, Youth and Under-21 level began his football career at Leeds United by joining a Youth Training Scheme. Though he failed to make the league side at Elland Road, he did appear in the Zenith Data Systems Cup match against Barnsley at Oakwell in November 1989, which Leeds won 2-1.

In the summer of 1991, Edwards had the choice of joining Black-

Neil Edwards

pool on a contract or Stockport County. Thankfully after seeking the advice of Mervyn Day and John Lukic, the Yorkshire club's senior 'keepers, he opted to join County. He made an impressive debut and kept a clean sheet in a 2-0 home win over Bury on 21st September 1991, and after only three games, County paid the Elland Road club £10,000 for his services.

An outstanding shot-stopper, Edwards played in 217 first team games for the Hatters before joining Rochdale in November 1997.

EMERSON, DEAN

Salford-born Dean Emerson opted to train as a screen printer rather than become a full-time apprentice footballer and so his first 23 games for the club following his debut at Bournemouth on 12th February 1982, were as a non-contract player. However, his displays over the remainder of that season were impressive and in May of that year, he signed full-time professional forms.

The red-haired midfielder was a virtual ever-present over the next three-and-a-half years, playing in 172 games out of 177, almost all of them in the number 4 shirt.

Because of the club's desperate financial position, it became inevitable that he would eventually leave Edgeley Park. He departed in the summer of 1985 after County had accepted Rotherham United's offer of £30,000 for the club's Player of the Year.

Dean Emerson

After just 15 months with the Millmoor club, Emerson was on the move again, this time to First Division Coventry City in an exchange deal worth £100,000. Immediately winning a first team place, he was unlucky to miss the Sky Blue's victory in the FA Cup Final of 1987 with a bad knee injury. After recovering, Emerson went on to make 132 first team appearances for the Highfield Road club before being given a free transfer.

He was quickly snapped up by Hartlepool United but after 60 appearances for the Third Division club he returned to Edgeley Park for a second spell. Finding County's midfield a different proposition from his earlier days with the club he made just 12 appearances before moving to Preston North End. He played in only two games for the Lilywhites before joining non-League Chorley.

EVER-PRESENTS

There have been 50 Stockport County players who have been ever-presents throughout a Football League season. The greatest number of ever-present seasons by a Stockport player is four by Bob Murray. Next in line come Harry Hardy, Trevor Porteous, Billy Haydock, John Rutter and Mike Flynn with three.

F

F.A. CUP

Stockport County first participated in the FA Cup in 1892-93, beating Halliwell Rovers 4-2 after extra-Time in the first qualifying round. This in fact was a replayed tie, the club's having met at Green Lane when Stockport won 4-0. Halliwell lodged a protest about the state of the ground and this appeal was upheld by the FA who ordered the tie to be replayed. The club were brought down to earth in the second round when they lost 8-1 at Bury.

In 1893-94, County became the first Combination club to reach the first round proper of the FA Cup. After a walk-over against Bootle, they beat Tranmere 2-1, Wrexham 7-0 and Crewe 2-1 after a replay before losing 1-0 at home to Burton Wanderers who were joining the Football League the next season.

County's best-ever FA Cup run came in 1934-35. After drawing 1-1 at Blyth Spartans, County won the replay 4-1 and were rewarded with a second round home tie against Darlington. With the score at 2-2 and just one minute remaining, County were awarded a penalty from which Bob Green scored to give the club a third round tie at West Ham. After a 1-1 draw at Upton Park, a Joe Hill goal gave County a 1-0 win in the replay and a fourth round meeting with Bradford City. After a goalless draw at Valley Parade, County won the replay 3-2 after extra-time to set up a fifth round meeting at Edgeley Park against First Division West Bromwich Albion. A new record crowd of 24,604 packed into the ground, but by half-time, County were 5-0 down and their glorious Cup run over.

The club reached the fifth round again in 1949-50 beating Gillingham (Home 3-0); Nottingham Forest (Away 2-0); Barnsley (Home 4-2) and Hull City (Away 2-0 after a goalless draw)) before being drawn at home to Liverpool. The club's highest recorded attendance of 27,833 saw the Reds win 2-1.

FATHER AND SON

On 5th May 1951, the final Saturday of the season, County's promising young 17-year-old forward, David Herd made his Football League debut against Hartlepool United. It was something of a unique event, because he and his father Alex became the first father and son to play alongside each other in a Football League match. David celebrated the occasion by scoring County's first goal in a 2-0 win.

FINNEY, KEN

Ken Finney played his early football with his home-town club St Helens and after a number of impressive performances, joined Stockport County in 1947. After making his debut in a 3-0 defeat at Lincoln City in January 1948, he played just nine more games in the next four seasons before winning a regular place at the start of the 1951-52 season.

Though he created a number of goal-scoring chances for the likes of Jack Connor and Bill Holden, he wasn't shot-shy and in 198 League and Cup games for County, he scored 36 goals with a best of 13 in 1956-57. Also during his stay at Edgeley Park, he represented the Third Division (North) against the Southern Section on two occasions.

In March 1958, Finney left Stockport to join Tranmere Rovers and in 195 League and Cup games for the Prenton Park club, scored 28 goals before signing for Altrincham.

FIRST DIVISION

After finishing runners-up to Bury in 1996-97, County embarked on their first season in the First Division. They didn't make the best of starts, drawing three and losing four of their first seven matches before beating Huddersfield Town 3-0. After that, the season proved to be very eventful with the club scoring 12 more goals than the previous season but also conceding goals at a fairly alarming rate on occasions. This is borne out in the following results – Sheffield United (Away 1-5), Reading (Home 5-1) and Wolverhampton Wanderers (Away 4-3). Despite a lot of changes on the playing side through long term injuries and player sales, the club finished in eighth place in the First Division thus achieving their highest-ever League placing. With Manchester City's relegation to the Second Division, County are now the second team in Greater Manchester!

FIRST LEAGUE MATCH

Stockport County played their first-ever Football League match on 1st September 1900. A crowd of around 7,000 attended the Leicester Fosse ground to see County playing in cerise and white shirts draw 2-2 with goals from Billy Betteley and Billy Smith, as twice they came from behind to equalise. The Stockport County team that day was: J.J.Moores; M.J.Earp; H.J.Wainwright; P.Pickford; A.J.Limond; B.Harvey; W.Betteley; W.J.Foster; J.Patterson; W.Smith; and H.Stansfield.

FLEWIN, REG

Centre-half Reg Flewin joined Portsmouth from Ryde Sports on the Isle of Wight and made his first team debut against Grimsby Town in May 1939. His playing career was badly affected by the war and though he appeared in 202 wartime games for Pompey, he only played in 169 League and Cup games in 18 years at the club.

He was Portsmouth's regular centre-half after the war and although a serious injury put him out of the side in January 1951, he had gained two League Championship medals as captain. He appeared for England in a wartime international and went on two FA tours to Canada in 1950 and Australia in 1951.

He retired from playing in 1953 and after a spell as youth team coach became the club's assistant manager. In October 1960, he left Fratton Park after 23 years to become his own boss with Stockport County.

He had three seasons of struggle at Edgeley Park in which the club finished 13th, 16th and 19th and if they hadn't won seven out of eight games late in the 1961-62 season, they would have finished even lower. He returned to the south coast in the summer of 1963 as manager of Bournemouth and in his first season almost led the Dean Court club to promotion to the Second Division when they finished fourth.

FLOODLIGHTS

County's floodlights were erected in 1956 and first used on 16th October, for a friendly against Dutch club Fortuna '54 Geleen. A crowd of 14,511 saw County go down 3-0, although there were complaints from the local Darts and Cribbage League that any future games played on Tuesday evening would be affected by the absence of darts players for whom that night had always been set aside!

FLYNN, MIKE

Born in Oldham, he joined his hometown club before a big money deal took him to the top flight with Norwich City. Things did not

Mike Flynn

work out for him as he had hoped at Carrow Road and he left without making a league appearance for the Canaries.

He signed for Preston North End in December 1990, for a fee of £125,000, making him at the time, the most expensive player in the Deepdale club's history. A cultured defender, he went on to play in 149 League and Cup games for North End before joining Stockport County for £150,000 in March 1993 – still the record transfer fee paid by the club.

He made his County debut as a substitute in a 4-3 win at Plymouth Argyle and in the last nine games of that 1992-93 season, he appeared in five different numbered shirts!

The club's only ever-present in 1993-94, he skippered County to the play-offs where they lost 2-1 to Burnley in the Wembley final. After finishing 11th in 1994-95, Flynn was again ever-present in the heart of County's defence in 1995-96 and again in 1996-97 when he led the club to promotion to the First Division and to the semi-finals of the League Cup.

A committed and fearless defender whose long throws also add to County's attacking options, he has now appeared in 263 first team games for the club.

FOGARTY, KEN

Defender Ken Fogarty was a determined competitor who never admitted defeat. The Manchester-born player made his County debut in a 2-1 home win over Darlington in March 1972, just days after his 17th birthday. He soon established himself in the first team and won honours as an Irish Youth international at 18 and became the club's youngest Player of the Year at the age of 19. He almost won a full cap for the Republic of Ireland when he was selected for the squad to play Poland. Unfortunately for Fogarty, Johnny Giles was appointed as manager and went for more experienced players.

After playing in 287 League and Cup games for the Edgeley Park club, he left for Fort Lauderdale Strikers in March 1979, in a £100,000 deal that also saw Terry Park cross the Atlantic.

FOOTBALL LEAGUE CUP

The Football League Cup was launched in 1960-61 and in their first-ever match, County beat Carlisle United 2-0 before travelling the short distance to Maine Road in the next round, where they were beaten 3-0. For the next six seasons, County went out of the competition at the first round stage and didn't win their next match until 28th August 1967, when they beat Crewe Alexandra 3-0 with Bill Atkins netting a hat-trick.

The club's best performance came in 1996-97 when the mighty Hatters reached the semi-final. Seeing off Premiership opposition in Blackburn Rovers, West Ham United and Southampton, County lost to Middlesborough 2-1 on aggregate, despite Sean Connelly giving them a 1-0 win at the Riverside Stadium.

County's best scoreline in the competition is the 5-2 defeat of Sheffield United at Bramall Lane on 24th September 1996, whilst they have also come in for one or two heavy defeats, namely 7-0 at Crystal Palace in 1979-80 and 7-0 against Sheffield Wednesday in 1986-87 in County's 'home' game played at Maine Road.

FORMATION

When Stockport County came into existence at the start of the 1890-91 season, it was in effect, nothing more than a change of title from Heaton Norris Rovers, that club being formed by a few young men of Wycliffe Congregational Chapel in 1883. They met round a table at McLaughlin's Temperance Bar and Restaurant, a well-known cafe close to Stockport town centre after deciding to 'get an association football team together'.

FOULKES, JABEZ

Known as 'Jabber', Foulkes played his early football with Fryston Colliery before joining Huddersfield Town in 1929. The Terriers were one of the strongest teams in the country at this time and right-winger Foulkes had to compete with Scottish international Alex Jackson for a first team spot. As a result, the Castleford-born player was given a free transfer and after impressing in a practice match at Edgeley Park, signed for County in the summer of 1932.

He made his debut for the Hatters on 27th August 1932, in a 5-1 victory over Darlington. A hardworking winger, he was a brilliant crosser of the ball and had the knack of scoring some very important goals.

He played a vital role in the 13-0 defeat of Halifax Town, setting up most of the goals and scoring one himself. He was an ever-present that season, scoring 13 goals and helping County to finish third in the Division. The club also reached the final of the Third Division (North) Cup, losing an exciting game 4-3 to Darlington at Old Trafford.

In his four seasons at Edgeley Park, Foulkes scored 37 goals in 162 appearances before leaving to join Bradford Park Avenue in the summer of 1936 for a fee of £2,000. He later ended his career with Halifax Town.

FOURTH DIVISION

Stockport County have had two spells in the Fourth Division. Their first from 1959-60 lasted eight seasons and in 1964-65 they had to seek re-election to the Football League after finishing bottom of the Fourth Division. Two seasons later, the club won the Fourth Division championship with 64 points, but lasted only three seasons in the Third Division before returning to the League's basement for the 1970-71 season.

County then spent the next 21 seasons in the Fourth Division, having to seek re-election in four of those campaigns before they finished runners-up to Darlington in 1990-91 to gain promotion to the Third Division.

FRAIN, DAVID

Though he signed schoolboy forms for Nottingham Forest, David Frain was not offered apprenticeship forms and so joined North East Counties League side, Dronfield United. After turning in a series of impressive performances, he was offered professional terms by his home-town club, Sheffield United. In two seasons at Bramall Lane, Frain only made 44 league appearances and when the then Rochdale manager Danny Bergara offered him the chance to join the Spotland club he did so.

When the Uruguayan became County's manager in 1989, Frain followed him to Edgeley Park. His transfer fee of £50,000, which was decided by a tribunal, was the club's record fee.

After making his debut in a 1-1 draw at home to Torquay United on 19th August 1989, Frain was soon sidelined by injury but recovered to become an important member of the club's midfield. He took over the captaincy in 1992 and led the Hatters out at Wembley, twice in the space of eight days. During the 1994-95 season he was loaned out to Mansfield Town before leaving Edgeley Park after playing in 243 games.

FRANCIS, KEVIN

Nicknamed 'Bigman', 'Inch' and 'Sir', Kevin Francis played for Mile Oak Rangers, a West Midlands Ansells Premier League side, before being taken on as a full-time professional by Derby County in 1988. In 1989-90 he made eight league appearances for the Rams, all of them as substitute when he occasionally linked up with Mick Harford and Dean Saunders. He failed to gain a regular place in the Derby side and after a couple of more substitute appearances, he was transferred to Stockport County in February 1991, for £45,000. He made his Stockport County debut as a substitute in a 3-0 win at Lincoln City before claiming five goals in his opening 13 league outings, helping them gain promotion from the Fourth Division.

Then in 1991-92, his presence was so vital as County stormed into the promotion play-offs in Division Three only to lose out at Wembley in the final to Peterborough United. In 1992-93, Francis scored a post-war record 39 goals including his first hat-trick for the club in a 4-3 win at Plymouth Argyle. In 1993-94 Francis netted 34 goals including another hat-trick in a 5-0 home win over Hartlepool United.

Though he is the league's tallest striker at 6ft 7ins, Francis ironically grabs more goals with his feet than he does with his head. Always a danger at set pieces he causes so much trouble in and around the opposing penalty area and invariably there always seems to be a scoring opportunity created when he gets into the box.

He left Edgeley Park in January 1995, after scoring 117 goals in 198 games to join Birmingham City for £800,000. Towards the end of his first season at St Andrews he suffered serious ligament damage and

Kevin Francis

though he played intermittently in 1995-96, again plagued by injury, he managed to score some spectacular goals. The 1996-97 season was no different and after scoring just 18 goals in 63 League and Cup games, he left Birmingham to try his luck with Oxford United.

FREIGHT ROVER TROPHY

A competition designed solely and specifically for the Associate Members of the Football League, the Freight Rover Trophy replaced the initial Associate Members Cup for the 1984-85 season.

After County had lost 5-1 at Burnley in the first round first leg, it didn't matter that they went down 1-0 at Edgeley Park in the return leg in front of a crowd of just 1,568.

In 1985-86, County lost 4-1 at Crewe Alexandra and though they drew 2-2 at home to Bolton Wanderers with both goals courtesy of Mark Leonard, who had also scored from the penalty spit at Gresty Road, it wasn't enough to take the club into the knockout stages.

In 1986-87, County again failed to qualify for the knockout stages, losing both preliminary round matches, 3-1 at Bury and 1-0 at home to Carlisle United.

FRYATT, JIM

Instantly recognisable with balding head and huge bushy sideburns, Jim Fryatt played for eight league clubs, three of them for two spells.

Signed by Charlton Athletic at the age of 17, the Southampton-born forward made only five appearances in three seasons at The Valley before signing for Southend United. Another three year spell in which he scored 24 goals in 61 games was followed by a move to Bradford Park Avenue. It was here that Fryatt scored a goal against Tranmere Rovers, that is credited as being the fastest ever, coming only four seconds after the kick-off. Fryatt scored 38 goals in 101 matches for the Yorkshire club over yet another three year spell before Southport took the proven goal-scorer to Haig Avenue.

A year later after 15 goals in 39 games, he was on the move again, this time to Torquay United but after just seven months on the Devon coast, in which he scored 11 goals in 27 outings, he joined Stockport County in October 1967, for £6,000.

He made his debut in a thrilling 4-3 home win over Southport in

Jim Fryatt

which he scored the opening goal. Forming a quite formidable partnership with Bill Atkins, he ended his first season at Edgeley Park as the club's top scorer with 22 goals including hat-tricks against Tranmere Rovers (Home 5-2) and Bristol Rovers (Home 3-1).

His goal-scoring exploits attracted interest from bigger clubs and after scoring six goals at the beginning of the following season, he joined Second Division Blackburn Rovers for £30,000. His time at Ewood Park was his least productive and 16 months later, he signed for Oldham Athletic for a fee of £8,000. He helped the Latics to win promotion from the Fourth Division, scoring 40 goals in 76 games before returning to Southport for a second spell and helping them win the Fourth Division championship in 1972-73.

In 1974 he returned to Edgeley Park for just one game, scoring his 189th and last league goal in a 3-2 home defeat by Rochdale.

He finished his league career with three more games for Torquay United before a short spell with non-League Chorley.

G

GALBRAITH, WALTER

After playing his early football with Clyde, Walter Galbraith joined New Brighton in 1948 before in August 1950, becoming player-manager. He lasted just a year with the Rakers as they finished bottom of the Third Division (North) and failed to gain re-election. He was signed as a player by Grimsby Town and in his first season helped the Mariners to runners-up spot in the Third Division (North). In June 1953, he became player-manager of Accrington Stanley, retiring from the playing side at the end of his first season at Peel Park. He stayed on as manager for another four seasons in which the club were twice runners-up and twice in third place – one of the best spells in their history. Because he had a policy of recruiting players from north of the border, he earned the tag of 'Mr McStanley'. Disappointed with the board's lack of ambition, he resigned in August 1958, but was back in work within three months as manager of Bradford Park Avenue. He later managed Tranmere Rovers but after they were relegated he moved back to Scotland to take charge at Hibernian. In 1965 he returned to Park Avenue as general manager before joining Stockport County as chief scout in the summer of 1968.

At the end of March 1969, he replaced Jimmy Meadows as manager but his one and only season in charge was nothing short of a disaster. Winning only six games, County finished bottom of the Third Division. Galbraith, however, was not given the chance to take the Edgeley Park club out of the League's basement, being sacked in April 1970.

GANNON, JIM

Though he was born in Southwark, Jim Gannon moved to Dublin with his family when he was 15 and played in an Irish FA Youth Cup Final before signing for Dundalk in 1985. During his three year stint with the Irish club he played in the European Cup against Red Star Belgrade before buying himself out of the Irish Permanent Defence Force in order to join Sheffield United for £50,000 in April 1989.

Jim Gannon

However, he was unable to break into the first team at Bramall Lane and made his Football League debut whilst on loan at Halifax Town.

In March 1990, County paid Sheffield United £70,000 to bring the defender to Edgeley Park. Though his first few months weren't particularly happy ones, his ability to play just behind the back four or in a defensive midfield role soon led to him winning over the supporters. Although Gannon is primarily a defender, he has scored his fair share of goals and in 1991-92 topped the club's league scoring charts with 16 goals including a hat-trick in a 4-1 home win over Exeter City.

He had just established a firm central defensive partnership with Mike Flynn when in December 1995, he broke his leg in a 2-0 home defeat by Shrewsbury Town and to make matters worse, he was booked by the referee as he was stretchered off the pitch!

One of County's longest serving players, the composed and effective defender has now appeared in 405 first team games for the club, scoring 64 goals.

GOALKEEPERS

Stockport County FC has almost always been extremely well served by its goalkeepers and most of them have been highly popular with the supporters.

The club's first outstanding 'keeper was Joe Butler who won a regular place during County's second season in the Football League. He went on to play in 190 League and Cup games in two spells with the club before returning to Edgeley Park in 1916 to play in the wartime League. In 1912-13 whilst playing for Sunderland, he won a League Championship medal and an FA Cup runners-up medal as Aston Villa beat the Roker Park club in the final.

One of County's most consistent goalkeepers was Harry Hardy, the club's only international player. He won his one and only cap in a 4-0 win over Belgium at The Hawthorns and during his time at Edgeley Park made 170 consecutive League appearances, his omission being as a result of his selection for the Football League.

Jack Bowles was one of County's most popular players. He was nicknamed 'Tiger' because the Cheltenham-born 'keeper always prowled the penalty area, crouching and waving his arms about, even when play was down at the other end of the field. He went on to appear in 306 first team games, the most by a County goalkeeper.

Ken Mulhearn and Alan Ogley were two goalkeepers of the highest order and whose careers continually crossed. Mulhearn kept goal for both Liverpool and Lancashire Schoolboys but when he was selected for the England Boys squad, he found his way barred by Alan Ogley. Mulhearn won a Fourth Division championship medal in 1967 before joining Manchester City for £25,000 plus Alan Ogley, who went on to give County eight tremendous seasons, only Jack Bowles having made more appearances as a County goalkeeper.

County goalkeeper Brian Lloyd scored from the edge of his own penalty area during the club's Fourth Division match at Bradford City in March 1982. That goal gave County a 1-0 lead but the popular 'keeper was beaten five times in the second-half as a blinding snow storm hampered the visitors.

GOALS

The most goals Stockport County have ever scored in one game was their 13-0 victory over Halifax Town in a Division Three (North) game at Edgeley Park on 6th January 1934. Percy Downes scored four, Joe Hill three, Alf Lythgoe and Jimmy Stevenson two goals apiece and one each from Jabez Foulkes and Eddie Vincent, who scored from the penalty-spot.

GOALS – CAREER BEST

The highest goal-scorer in the club's history is Jack Connor who between season 1951-52 and the end of season 1956-57, netted 140 goals for the club. These comprised of 132 in the League and eight in the FA Cup.

GOALS – INDIVIDUAL

Five players have scored five goals in a game for Stockport County in the Football League and one of them, Joe Smith, performed the feat on two occasions. He first netted five goals in a 6-3 home win over Southport on 7th January 1928, and repeated the feat the following season as County beat Lincoln City 7-3 at Edgeley Park on 15th September 1928. The second player to achieve the feat was Frank Newton who scored five goals, including a penalty in County's 6-1 home success over Nelson on 21st September 1929. During Alf Lythgoe's record breaking season of 1933-34 when he scored 46 League goals, he scored four goals on two occasions before netting five on the opening day of the following season as County beat Southport 6-1. On 14th December 1935, Billy McNaughton scored five of Stockport's goals in a 6-1 home win over Mansfield Town. The last player to score five goals was Jack Connor on 7th April 1956, as Carlisle United were beaten 8-1.

GOALS – SEASON

The club's highest League goal-scorer in any one season is Alf Lythgoe who scored 46 League goals as County finished third in Division Three (North) in 1933-34. He scored four goals on two occasions: Southport (home 9-2) and Wrexham (Home 7-3) and hat-tricks against Darlington (home 6-0); Southport (Away 4-1) and Mansfield Town (Home 3-1).

GOAL-SCORING RECORDS

Stockport County have scored in every League game at home during a season on only two occasions, in 1907-08 and in 1928-29. Yet there have been 11 seasons when the club have gone goalless in only one home game, the last time being 1977-78.

GOODWIN, FRED

Fred Goodwin began his League career with Wolverhampton Wanderers and made his debut for the Molineux club in the First Division in the early 1960s. Around this time, he was chosen to play for England Youth against West Germany Youth but because Wolves were involved in a FA Youth Cup semi-final against Chelsea, he was denied permission to play. Wolves won through to the final but lost 2-0 to Newcastle United. Goodwin played in 44 games for Wolves before joining Stockport County on a free transfer in January 1966.

After making his debut for the Hatters at inside-forward in a 4-2 home defeat by Wrexham, Goodwin went on to appear in every position for his home-town club – including goalkeeper, when he replaced the injured Alan Ogley at Orient in February 1968.

The following season whilst playing centre-forward he scored four goals against the same opponents as County won 5-2 at Edgeley Park. In March 1970, with the club already doomed to relegation, Goodwin was transferred to Blackburn Rovers after making 206 League and Cup appearances.

After a couple of seasons at Ewood Park, Goodwin joined former County boss Jimmy Meadows at Southport before later playing for Port Vale. After a brief spell with Macclesfield Town, he returned to Edgeley Park on a month to month contract. He played in a further 20 games before ligament problems forced him to retire from League football. He then coached at a number of non-League clubs before emigrating to New Zealand. He spent 13 years coaching in New Zealand and was assistant-coach to the national team before returning to Stockport in 1993.

GRIFFITHS, JOHN

As a boy, John Griffiths was an all-round sportsman, playing cricket and football for Worcestershire Boys and winning medals for cross-country running and swimming. On leaving school, he spent three months as a trainee draughtsman before signing apprentice forms with Aston Villa.

Despite the fact that he finished top scorer in Villa's Reserve team for two years running, his first team appearances were limited to just three before he joined County in June 1970. Though he made his debut in the opening game of the 1970-71 season, a goalless draw at home to Peterborough United, he had to wait until his 34th appearance before he scored his first goal for the club, the winner in a 2-1 win at Scunthorpe United in April 1971. The following season he played in the unaccustomed position of outside-left but in 1972-73 he reverted to centre-forward and had his best season for the club, top scoring with 13 goals in the League. Over the next few seasons he went on to make 201 League and Cup appearances, scoring 31 goals before being released at the end of the 1974-75 season.

GUEST PLAYERS

The 'guest' system was used by all clubs during the two wars. Although at times it was abused almost beyond belief (in that some sides that opposed County had ten or 11 'guests'!) it normally worked sensibly and effectively to the benefit of players, clubs and supporters alike.

During the First World War, former County favourites Bob Suart from Port Vale and goalkeeper Jimmy Molyneux from Chelsea 'guested' for County as did Watford's Tommy Waterall (the brother of Stockport's Albert) and 'Tiny' Fayers, the Huddersfield Town centre-half.

The most distinguished players to 'guest' for County during the Second World War were Harry Catterick junior of Everton, who scored 98 goals in 122 games, Tommy G. Jones also of Everton, Willie Hall of Spurs and England, the Manchester United trio of Jack Crompton, William Bryant and George Vose and Sammy Weaver of Chelsea and England who joined the club on a permanent basis in December 1945.

H

HARDY, HARRY

The only player capped for his country while at Edgeley Park, goalkeeper Harry Hardy played for England in a 4-0 win over Belgium at The Hawthorns in December 1924. Replacing Joseph Bird who had conceded eight goals in the opening two games of the 1920-21 season – Cardiff City (Home 2-5) and Fulham (Away 1-3) – Hardy made his debut in the return match at Cardiff but could do little to reverse the trend as County lost 3-0. However, he retained his place in the side and went on to make 170 consecutive league appearances for County from his debut. The reason he missed the next game came as a result of his selection for the Football League against the Irish League on 11th October 1924, the day County entertained Southampton.

In 1921-22 when the Edgeley Park club won the Third Division (North) championship, Hardy kept 23 clean sheets. He went on to appear in 214 League and Cup games for County before joining Everton for £2,350 in October 1925.

His first two games for the Goodison Park club saw him concede seven goals as the Toffees lost to Arsenal (Away 1-4) and Manchester United (Home 1-3). When Everton won the League Championship in 1927-28, Hardy played in just six games, leaving at the end of the season to join Bury. He made 27 appearances for the Shakers before hanging up his boots.

HART, PAUL

The son of the former Manchester City forward and manager, Johnny Hart, Paul began his league career with Stockport County and made his debut in a 4-3 home win over Lincoln City in October 1970. The fol-

Paul Hart

lowing two seasons, Hart was a virtual ever-present in the County side and though the club were going through a bad patch, his performances stood out, so much so, that in the summer of 1973 he was sold to Blackpool for £25,000.

His reputation grew at Bloomfield Road where he was an ever-present in 1976-77 but with the Seasiders' relegation to the Third Division virtually assured he joined Leeds United for £300,000. He made over 200 appearances for the Elland Road club before moving to Nottingham Forest in the 1983 close season. Two years later he joined Sheffield Wednesday but despite adding authority to the Owls' back four, he was transferred to Birmingham City. Sadly, he broke his leg on his debut and never appeared again for the St Andrews' club.

In the summer of 1987 he joined Notts County as player-coach, later managing Chesterfield to a Wembley play-off final.

HARTFORD, ASA

Named after the celebrated American singer Al Jolson, Asa Hartford was plucked from Scottish amateur football after being spotted by a West Bromwich Albion scout. He was soon thrilling the crowds with his mature skill and vision and it was only a matter of time before the inevitable big money offer arrived to tempt Albion.

Hartford will probably always be remembered as the player whose transfer to Leeds United was sensationally called off after a routine medical examination revealed a hole-in-the-heart condition. That was in 1972, but two years later he joined Manchester City for £225,000 and went on to play a major role in City's glamorous era of the late 1970s, picking up a League Cup winners' medal with them in 1976.

In June 1979, he joined Brian Clough's Nottingham Forest but after only 63 days and three league games, he was on his way back to the north-west and Everton. After two seasons at Goodison, the Scottish international who won 50 caps returned to Maine Road for a second spell. After 318 first team games and 36 goals, Hartford crossed the Atlantic to join the ranks of Fort Lauderdale Sun. He later returned to top flight action with Norwich City, helping them win the Milk Cup in 1985, when his shot was deflected by Sunderland's Chisholm for the only goal of the game. He then joined Bolton Wanderers where he became club captain and a great inspiration.

Asa Hartford

In the summer of 1987 he joined Stockport County as player-manager and though he made some impressive signings, the club could only finish 20th in the Fourth Division. In March 1989, with no real improvement having been made, he went to manage Shrewsbury. He then worked for Blackburn and Stoke before returning to Maine Road for a third time as Alan Ball's second-in-command.

HAT-TRICK HEROES

The scorer of the club's first hat-trick in the Football League was **William Foster** who scored all four goals in a 4-1 home win over Walsall on 22nd September 1900, in only the club's fifth game.

In 1927-28, **Joe Smith** scored 40 goals in 42 League and Cup games including four hat-tricks in the space of seven games. When he left Edgeley Park in the summer of 1929 the former Bolton and England international had scored 63 goals in 73 League and Cup games including eight hat-tricks!

Former Wolves centre-forward **Joe Griffiths** scored all three goals on his debut in a 3-2 home win over York City on 23rd January 1932.

During the 1933-34 season, **Alf Lythgoe** netted five hat-tricks, including one in a three-minute spell against Southport on 4th November 1933. He also scored a hat-trick of hat-tricks in March 1934 – Darlington (Home 6-0); Southport (Away 4-1) and Wrexham (Home 7-3).

When County lost 3-0 to Lincoln City on 16th September 1935, all the Sincil Bank club's goals were scored by their captain Horne and all from the penalty-spot!

When **Len Barker** made his County debut on 28th August 1948, he scored all three goals in a 3-3 draw at Crewe Alexandra, after the Edgeley Park club had trailed 0-3.

Jack Connor holds the club record for the most hat-tricks with 17 which included four goals in games against Bradford Park Avenue (Home 6-0 in 1954-55) and Tranmere Rovers (Home 7-0 in 1955-56) and five goals against Workington (Home 6-0 in 1952-53) and Carlisle United (Home 8-1 in 1955-56). In 1953 he emulated Alf Lythgoe's record of scoring a hat-trick of hat-tricks.

Les Bradd scored a remarkable hat-trick in the match against

Barnsley at Oakwell on 24th February 1979. With just ten minutes remaining, the Yorkshire side were leading 4-1 but Bradd netted a hat-trick in the space of seven minutes to give County a 4-4 draw

HAYDOCK, BILLY

After playing for Eccles Boys, Billy Haydock joined his brother Frank at Manchester United but unable to force his way into the first team, left to join Blackpool. Though he was offered professional terms at Bloomfield Road, he turned them down in order to finish his apprenticeship as a motor engineer. He then joined Cheshire League side Buxton, where he was spotted by Manchester City, who paid £2,500 for his services, a record for the Derbyshire club.

In two and a half years at Maine Road, the versatile Haydock made only three appearances, before he and Jim Pennington were allowed to move to Crewe Alexandra for a combined fee of £7,000.

When Crewe manager and former County player Jimmy McGuigan moved to Grimsby Town, Haydock followed him for a fee of £5,000. After only 21 appearances for the Mariners, he moved to Edgeley Park, this time for £4,000.

Though he was classed as a utility player, playing as an inside-forward, full-back or mostly wing-half, he was successfully switched to right-back and over the next six seasons went on to play in 287 League and Cup games for the Hatters. He was an ever-present in 1966-67 when County won the Fourth Division championship. After being released at the end of the 1970-71 season he saw out his playing career in this country with Southport before playing and coaching at Port Elizabeth in South Africa.

On his return to these shores he became Blackpool's physiotherapist. After being promoted to first team coach at Bloomfield Road, he went abroad to manage ASK Vikinger in Iceland followed by ASK Tromso in Norway. He continued his travels by working as coach to Cork City in Ireland before returning briefly to Edgeley Park as the club's physiotherapist. When County boss Asa Hartford moved to Shrewsbury, Haydock followed him. On Hartford's dismissal, Haydock coached in Norway and Canada but linked up with Hartford again as second team physiotherapist at Blackburn Rovers.

HERD, ALEX

After beginning his career with Hamilton Academicals, Alex Herd made a dramatic entry into English football, for within 15 months, he had played in two FA Cup Finals for Manchester City. A member of one of the club's greatest-ever teams, he starred in the 1936-37 side which won the League Championship, making 32 appearances and scoring 15 goals. A deep-lying inside-forward, Alex Herd's career stretched into wartime football and in 1942 he was capped by Scotland. When peacetime football resumed, Herd was still at Maine Road and won a Second Division championship medal in 1946-47.

Herd left City for Stockport County on a free transfer in March 1948, and proved a valuable acquisition for the Edgeley Park club. In 1949-50, he was the club's top scorer with 19 League and Cup goals, including four in their historic FA Cup run. On the last day of the 1950-51 season, he turned out alongside his son David when they were County's inside-forwards against Hartlepool United.

Alex Herd went on to score 41 goals in 119 League and Cup games, playing his last game against New Brighton on Christmas Day 1951 at the age of 40 years 47 days.

HILL, JOE

Joe Hill began his career with Leeds United but after failing to win a first team place joined Barnsley. He had scored three goals in eight games for the Oakwell club when he moved to Queen's Park Rangers in the summer of 1932. After one season at Loftus Road, he returned north to join Stockport County, though he had to wait until Boxing Day 1933 before making a goal-scoring debut in a 2-2 draw at Carlisle United.

Hill made his home debut in the 13-0 victory over Halifax Town and scored a hat-trick. Even so, it was 1934-35 before he won a regular place in the County side, scoring 16 goals in 45 League and Cup games. In 1935-36 he was the club's top scorer with 19 goals, a feat he repeated the following season as County won the Third Division (North) championship. His total of 21 league goals included a hat-trick in a 4-0 home win over Chester.

Hill went on to score 71 goals in 154 League and Cup games for County before joining Walsall in 1938.

HODDER, KEN

A solid and reliable centre-half, Ken Hodder made his first team debut in a 2-1 win at Halifax Town in March 1952, following an injury to Gordon Wilmott. However, he had to wait until 1955-56 before he became a regular member of County's first team.

During the early part of the 1957-58 season, Hodder lost his place in the side and missed all of the following campaign before winning his place back in October 1959. It was the start of his best spell for the club as he played in 101 consecutive League and Cup games. He was an ever-present in 1960-61, when he scored his only goal for the club from the penalty spot in a 1-0 win over Doncaster Rovers at Edgeley Park. Unfortunately for the popular defender he broke his leg in a reserve game at Middlesbrough in September 1963, and was forced to give up the game after making 272 League and Cup appearances for the club.

He remained at Edgeley Park coaching the club's apprentices before leaving to start his own decorating business.

HOLDEN, BILL

One of the many professional footballers to come out of Folds Road School, Bolton, Bill Holden was spotted playing for the Dobson and Barlow works team by Everton and offered a trial. He was unsuccessful at Goodison Park but was later seen by Jack Marshall, Burnley's former player and scout in the Bolton area and signed for the Clarets as an amateur in September 1949.

He was soon into his goal-scoring stride and emerged as Burnley's top scorer during 1950-51, his first season as a professional. He went on to win England 'B' honours and in six seasons at Turf moor, scored 79 goals in 199 League and Cup outings.

Sunderland took Holden to Roker Park at Christmas 1955 for a fee of £12,000. Although he scored after just four minutes of his debut match against Newcastle United, he never really settled on Wearside and after less than a year, joined Stockport County for £6,000.

In his only full season with County, 1957-58, he top-scored with 17 goals, netting his first hat-trick for the club on 2nd November 1957, as County beat Chesterfield 4-1. He was the club's top scorer again the following season but in March 1959, with County heading for relegation to the Fourth Division, he joined Bury with Jimmy Reid and Bill Ritchie moving in the opposite direction.

His goals played a big part in Bury's Third Division championship success in 1960-61, but after one more season at Gigg Lane, he joined Halifax in the summer of 1962, ending his League career at The Shay. He later played non-League football for Rugby Town and Hereford United.

HOME MATCHES

Stockport County's best home wins are the 13-0 rout of Halifax Town on 6th January 1934, which is a joint League record victory and the 9-2 defeat of Southport two months earlier. The club's worst home defeat, although the match was played at Maine Road was the 7-0 beating handed out by Sheffield Wednesday in a second round second leg League Cup tie.

County have scored eight goals in a home match on three occasions – Nelson 8-0 (Division Three (North) in 1927-28), Chester 8-5 (Division Three (North) in 1932-33) and Carlisle United 8-1 (Division Three (North) in 1955-56).

HOME SEASONS

Stockport County have gone through a complete League season with an undefeated home record on three occasions – 1927-28, 1928-29 and 1933-34. The club's highest number of home wins in a League season is 19. This was achieved in 1928-29 from 21 matches as they finished runners-up in the Third Division (North).

HONOURS

The major honours achieved by the club are:

   Champions Third Division (North): 1921-22 and 1936-37
   Champions Fourth Division: 1966-67
   Lancashire League: 1899-1900
   Division Three (North) Cup: 1934-35
   Autoglass Trophy Finalists: 1991-92 and 1992-93

HUNDRED GOALS

The Hatters have scored more than 100 League goals in a season on three occasions. The highest total is 115 goals scored in 1933-34 when they finished third in the Third Division (North). In 1928-29 they scored 111 goals and the season after, 106 goals, finishing runners-up in the Third Division (North) on both occasions.

HYDE, LINCOLN

Lincoln Hyde made a goal-scoring debut for Stockport County in a 3-1 win against Lincoln City at Sincil Bank in December 1913, to provide the newspapers with the dream headline of 'Lincoln beats Lincoln at Lincoln'. He went on to make 13 League appearances before the outbreak of the First World War and appeared in nine wartime games.

He was appointed manager at Edgeley Park in June 1926, and immediately appointed Fred Westgarth as trainer. Hyde often had to sell players in order to pay his way but he had the happy knack of finding men capable to fill the gaps.

Hyde was very unlucky not to get County promoted. They finished third in 1927-28 and were runners-up in the next two seasons in the Third Division (North) but in those days only the champions were promoted. He succeeded in producing attractive high-scoring teams and in each of the last two seasons they scored over 100 goals and gained over 60 points.

In April 1931, he accepted the offer of the manager's job at Preston North End but he was never given complete control in his time at Deepdale. The directors decided who was bought and sold and Hyde lasted just one season as North End struggled near the foot of the Second Division.

I

INTERNATIONAL PLAYERS

County's only ever international player was goalkeeper Harry Hardy who after a number of impressive displays at Edgeley Park, made his one and only full appearance for England against Belgium at West Bromwich in December 1924. For the record, Hardy kept a clean sheet in a 4-0 win for England.

J

JACKSON, ARNOLD

Inside-forward Arnold Jackson began his League career with Shrewsbury Town and in four seasons at Gay Meadow, scored 45 goals in 153 League and Cup games.

He joined County in the summer of 1954 and made his debut in a 5-2 home win over Carlisle United on the opening day of the 1954-55 season. He scored 11 goals in 39 league games in that campaign but over the next two seasons he was not an automatic choice and only became a first team regular in 1957-58. During that season he scored 16 League and Cup goals including all three in a 3-3 home draw against Mansfield Town.

Though he was overshadowed in the goal-scoring stakes by Jack Connor, he netted 52 goals in 162 League and Cup games in his five seasons at Edgeley Park.

JEFFERS, JOHN

Unable to break into Liverpool's first team, Jeffers left Anfield to join Port Vale on loan in December 1988, before eventually signing for the Valiants for £30,000 in March 1989.

A tricky winger with a superb left foot, he created a number of goals for Beckford and Futcher, playing his part in the club's promotion after their play-off success over Bristol Rovers in June 1989. Despite suffering with a series of stomach problems, he continued to impress and in 1993-94, his pin-point crosses provided Martin Foyle with many of his goals.

In January 1995, he joined Shrewsbury Town on loan and after a trial with Stockport County at the beginning of the following season, he joined the Edgeley Park club on a free transfer. The Liverpool-born winger had played in 219 games for Vale, scoring 11 goals.

He made his County debut in a 1-1 draw at home to Swindon Town

John Jeffers

in November 1995. Making an immediate impact he gave the side
more balance and in 1996-97 was instrumental in the club's run to the
League Cup semi-finals and their push for promotion to the First Division.

JENKINSON, FRED

After leaving Barnsley Grammar School, Fred Jenkinson followed his
father down the mines, whilst playing amateur football for Intake
WMC. Able to play in either of the full-back positions, Jenkinson
joined Stockport County in December 1930. He didn't make his first
team debut until the opening game of the 1931-32 season, a 1-1 draw
at Doncaster Rovers and in fact, didn't win a regular place until the
following season when County were third in Division Three (North).

An ever-present in 1933-34 and 1935-36, he missed just one game in 1936-37 when the club won the Third Division (North) championship. His only goal for the club came in the following season's Second Division campaign as County beat Tottenham Hotspur 3-2 on 2 October 1937.

During his eight seasons at Edgeley Park, Jenkinson had the chance to join Wolverhampton Wanderers, but thankfully turned the opportunity down and went on to make 295 appearances for the club before retiring to run a guest house in Bournemouth.

JOBSON, JACK

Jack Jobson began his career with Plymouth Argyle before returning to his native north-east to play for Hartlepool United. He joined Stockport County in the summer of 1927 and played his first game for the club in a 2-0 home win over Rotherham United on the opening day of the 1927-28 season.

He went on to become the club's first-choice centre-half for the next five seasons, appearing in 181 League and Cup games and scoring seven goals. During his stay at Edgeley Park, the team finished

Dave Jones

runners-up in the Third Division (North) in consecutive seasons and were desperately unlucky not to win promotion.

In June 1932, Jobson left Stockport to sign for Queen's Park Rangers but after a year at Loftus Road, he returned to the north-east where he saw out his career with Gateshead.

JONES, DAVE

Dave Jones' career as a footballer was cut short by an injury after an England Under-21 cap and a promising start to his club career with Everton and Coventry City.

As a manager, Jones worked his way up from the bottom. He was with Morecambe, Southport and Mossley before moving to Edgeley Park, first as coach. Though he was appointed County manager in March 1995 following the departure of Danny Bergara, Jones only signed a manager's contract in February 1997!

In his first full season in charge, Jones took the club to the semi-finals of the Football League Cup and to promotion to the First Division as runners-up to Bury. Not surprisingly, he was named as the Division Two's Manager of the Year, yet at the start of the season, there were those who would have let him move on.

At the end of June 1997, Jones was appointed manager of Premier League Southampton. His first move was to get Matthew Le Tissier to sign a new four-year contract. Jones has been an inspirational choice for the Saints, especially when one considers the appointments at one or two of the bigger clubs in 1997-98.

JONES, LEN

Though he was born in Birkenhead, Len Jones was only a couple of weeks old when his family moved back to Holywell in North Wales and explains why he played in two amateur internationals for Wales!

After playing for Holywell and Flint, he had a spell with Huddersfield Town before joining Rhyl. He signed for Stockport County in the summer of 1933 and made his debut at left-half in a 4-2 defeat at Halifax Town on 2nd September 1933. Midway through the following season, he was switched to centre-half and over the next four campaigns, missed very few games, being ever-present in 1936-37.

It was during this season that Jones scored his only goal for the club in the 2-1 win at Crewe as County won the Third Division (North) championship. He played in 226 League and Cup games before a leg injury forced his retirement from the game.

K

KELLY, BOB

A former miner, Bob Kelly was a very skilful player who played his early football with Burnley. He made almost 300 League and Cup appearances for the Turf Moor club, scoring 97 goals, although he missed the club's FA Cup triumph over Liverpool in 1914. In 1920-21 he won a League Championship medal, playing in 27 of the 30 consecutive unbeaten matches that they achieved that season. Kelly, who had a deadly shot, excellent dribbling skills and a fine body swerve, later played for Sunderland, Huddersfield Town and Preston North End, where in his second season, he helped the Deepdale club to promotion to the First Division.

At the age of 40, the England international joined Carlisle United as player-manager but in November 1936, he took charge at Edgeley Park. At the end of his first season, County won the Third Division (North) championship but were relegated straight back again the following season, after which Kelly resigned.

KENNY, FRED

Unable to break into Manchester City's first team, Fred Kenny joined Stockport County in December 1947, but had to wait nine months before making his debut in a 3-1 home win over Gateshead. In 1949-50, Kenny was badly injured and over the next two seasons, only appeared in five games. He fought his way back to full fitness and in 1951-52 when the Hatters were third in Division Three (North) he was the club's only ever-present.

He went on to appear in 214 League and Cup games for the Edgeley Park club, his final match being against New Brighton in a first round FA Cup match in November 1956, which ended all-square at 3-3. On leaving Stockport, Kenny had a brief spell as manager of Cheadle Town.

L

LANCASHIRE COMBINATION

After failing to win re-election to the Football League, County applied for entry to the Lancashire Combination for the 1904-05 season. They began the season with four straight wins but on 29th October 1904, after the club had won seven of its first eight games they were required to play an FA Cup match against Stalybridge Rovers and a Lancashire Combination match against Bolton Wanderers Reserves. Because the club needed the revenue they fielded their first team in the Cup match and played 11 entirely different players in the League. They lost 3-1 at Bolton, one of only five defeats in a season which saw them go on to win the Lancashire Combination championship and election to the Second Division of the Football League.

LANCASHIRE LEAGUE

With the Lancashire League extending its membership to 14 clubs for the 1894-95 season, County decided to leave the Combination and play in a higher standard of football. The club drew its first match 2-2 at home to Chorley and over the season held their own against much stronger opposition than they had met in their Combination days to finish the campaign in ninth place. In 1895-96, the League was extended to 16 clubs but County suffered a disappointing season and finished 12th. However, they did beat the leaders Nelson 4-0 at home with George Smith scoring a hat-trick. The following season saw the club finish ninth out of 15 clubs, a satisfactory position after County had lost six of their opening eight matches.

The Lancashire League changed dramatically for the start of the 1897-98 season with five new teams entering the competition. County enjoyed their best season to date and in the New Year strung together a run of seven consecutive League wins in which they scored 28 goals. Unfortunately, they fell away towards the end of the season and had to be content with third place. In 1898-99, County slipped to a disappointing sixth place but made amends the following season.

In 1899-1900, County won their first four games of the season and though they then lost two of their next five games, they enjoyed a run of 11 games without defeat to go top of the table. Despite a 4-1 defeat at Blackpool, County won their next six games to win the Championship and election to Division Two of the Football League.

LARGEST CROWD

It was on 11th February 1950, that Edgeley Park housed its largest crowd. The occasion was the FA Cup fifth round match against Liverpool. A crowd of 27,833 saw County lose 2-1 with Alex Herd scoring for the Hatters.

LATE FINISHES

Stockport's final match of the season against York City at Edgeley Park on 31st May 1947, is the latest date for the finish of any County season. For the record, goals from Dainty (2), Earl and Jessop helped the Hatters to a 4-2 win.

LATE, LATE SHOW

On 28th November 1953, Crewe Alexandra were leading Stockport County 1-0 in a Third Division (North) game at Gresty Road with under 30 minutes remaining. County went on to win 5-1 with Jack Connor, who later joined the Railwaymen, scoring a hat-trick.

LAWTHER, IAN

Belfast-born Ian Lawther began his career in Northern Ireland for Crusaders where he was spotted by Sunderland manager Alan Brown. He signed for the then Roker Park club in March 1958, but couldn't prevent the Wearsiders from being relegated to the Second Division.

Capped at full international level, he scored 32 goals for Sunderland in 1960-61 before being transferred to Blackburn Rovers in the close season. He scored 21 goals in 59 league appearances for the

Ewood Park club before joining Scunthorpe United two years later. He had a similar record with the Irons before moving to Brentford, the Griffin Park club giving him his longest spell at one club so far. He scored 43 goals in 139 games for the Bees before signing for Halifax Town in the summer of 1968.

In his first season at The Shay, he helped the Yorkshire club to their first-ever promotion and in his second and last season with the club almost led them to Second Division football.

Joining County in July 1971, he made his debut in a 3-1 defeat at Crewe on the opening day of the 1971-72 season before scoring both goals in a 2-2 draw at home to Bury in the next game. He ended the season as the club's top scorer with 13 goals, including a hat-trick in a 3-1 home win over Crewe Alexandra. He ended the following season as the club's joint top-scorer before being switched to centre-half for the start of the 1973-74 campaign. Having been made captain, he went on to score 34 goals in 183 League and Cup games for County before retiring in 1976.

LEADING GOAL-SCORERS

Stockport County have provided the leading goal-scorer in a division of the Football League on six occasions:

Joe Smith	1927-28	Third Division (North)	38 goals
Frank Newton	1929-30	Third Division (North)	36 goals
Alf Lythgoe	1933-34	Third Division (North)	46 goals
Jack Connor	1953-54	Third Division (North)	31 goals
Jack Connor	1954-55	Third Division (North)	30 goals*
Brett Angell	1989-90	Fourth Division	23 goals

* Joint top-scorer

LEAGUE GOALS - CAREER HIGHEST

Jack Connor holds the Edgeley Park record for the most league goals with a career total of 140 goals between 1951 and 1956.

LEAGUE GOALS – LEAST CONCEDED

During the 1921-22 season, County conceded just 21 goals in 38 games when winning the Third Division (North) championship.

LEAGUE GOALS – MOST CONCEDED

During the 1925-26 season, County conceded 97 goals in 42 games when finishing bottom of the Second Division and were relegated to the Third Division (North).

LEAGUE GOALS – MOST INDIVIDUAL

Alf Lythgoe holds the Stockport County record for the most League goals in a season with 46 scored in the Third Division (North) during the 1933-34 season.

LEONARD, MARK

Born in St Helens, Mark Leonard joined Everton from Witton Albion in February 1982, but failed to make the grade with the Goodison club and made his league debut in a 1-0 defeat at Darlington a year later, whilst on loan at Tranmere Rovers.

At the end of the 1982-83 season, he moved to Crewe Alexandra on a free transfer and in 60 League and Cup games for the Railwaymen scored 17 goals. He joined County in February 1985, and made his debut in a 2-1 home defeat by Southend United.

In 1985-86, Leonard was the club's top scorer with 23 League and Cup goals including six doubles, as they finished 11th in the Fourth Division. He went on to score 28 goals in 81 games for the Edgeley Park club before joining Bradford City for a fee of £40,000 in September 1986. Though many of his first team appearances for the Valley Parade club were as a substitute, he netted 39 goals in 195 games before moving to Rochdale for a similar fee in March 1992. His stay at Spotland was short and five months later he joined Preston North End, again for a fee of £40,000.

After just one season at Deepdale he was on the move again, this time to Chester City before joining Wigan Athletic in September 1994. At Springfield Park, this enthusiastic traditional centre-

Mark Leonard

forward netted 16 goals in 78 first team games before returning to Rochdale for a second spell.

LEWIS, HARRY

A genial and unassuming man, Harry Lewis replaced Fred Stewart as County manager in June 1911. His stay at Edgeley Park lasted three seasons, one of which in 1912-13 they had to apply for re-election for the first time since their return to the Football League in 1905.

He left the club in April 1914, to become manager of Barnsley and in his first season at Oakwell, he led the club to third in Division Two. He left Barnsley before the resumption of post-war football, becoming Hull City manager in the summer of 1921. But things became strained at Anlaby Road when the Hull board instituted a selection committee to pick the team for him. Lewis resigned after a poor 1922-23 season and though this was his last managerial position, he did advise Rotherham County in their early years in the Football League.

LEYLAND DAF CUP

The Leyland Daf Cup replaced the Sherpa Van Trophy for the 1989-90 season. The club won its first match in this variously-named competition at the twelfth time of asking, winning 2-0 at Burnley with goals from Beaumont and Angell. Despite going down 4-2 at home to Preston North End, County qualified for the knockout stages and in the first round beat Carlisle United at Brunton Park, 2-1 after extra-time. The club's second round tie also went to extra-time but on this occasion County lost 3-1 to Halifax Town.

In 1990-91, the club drew both preliminary round matches at Crewe Alexandra and at home to Burnley 1-1 and so qualified for the knockout stages where they played the Clarets again, only this time at Turf Moor. In an exciting game, County lost 3-2 after extra-time.

LINCOLN, ANDY

Having played his early football with Millwall and Northampton Town, inside-forward Andy Lincoln joined County in the summer of 1929 and immediately formed a formidable striking partnership with Frank Newton. After making his debut in a 1-1 draw at Wrexham on the opening day of the season, he scored a hat-trick on his home debut in a 5-0 win over Barrow. Between 25th January and 8th March 1930, he established a club record by scoring in nine successive league matches and finished the season with 28 League and Cup goals.

In 1930-31 he scored 14 goals including another hat-trick against Barrow in a 6-0 home win. Having scored 42 goals in 86 League and Cup appearances, he joined the club of his name, Lincoln City before ending his career with Gateshead.

LLOYD, BRIAN

A former Welsh international goalkeeper, Brian Lloyd is the only County Number One ever to score a goal in a Football League match. It came in the first half of a Fourth Division match at Bradford City on 10th March 1982, and gave County a half-time lead, though in the second period, the Bantams put five goals past the Rhyl-born 'Keeper!

Brian Lloyd

Lloyd was signed from his home-town club in March 1967, as cover for Steve Fleet and Ken Mulhearn, making his debut in a 1-1 draw at Colchester United in April 1968. The following season he shared the goalkeeping duties with Alan Ogley but at the beginning of the 1969-70 campaign, the club accepted a £10,000 offer from Southend United. He never really settled at Roots Hall and after two seasons he moved back to Wales and Wrexham in the Third Division.

It was whilst at the Racecourse Ground that Lloyd ran up a club record 312 consecutive matches in all competitions and made his three appearances for the national side. His debut for Wales came in a 1-0 win over Austria at the Racecourse Ground.

In September 1977, he joined Chester, where he made 94 appearances before 16 games on loan to Port Vale led to a return to Edgeley Park in the summer of 1981. Missing only one match in the next two seasons, he played his 500th league match in a 1-1 draw with Peterborough United at Edgeley Park on 28th August 1982. At the end of that season, Lloyd retired from first-class football after appearing in 133 games in his two spells with the club.

LONGEST GAME

When the Division Three (North) wartime Cup tie between Stockport County and Doncaster Rovers on 30th March 1946, ended in a draw after extra-time, the two sides were asked to settle the outcome on that day. The first team to score would win. But the scores were still level after 203 minutes when the game was abandoned through bad light.

The Cup tie had two legs. The first at Doncaster ended in a 2-2 draw. The second at Stockport finished with the same 2-2 scoreline. The competition rules dictated extra-time of ten minutes each way. This was played with no scoring. The teams then played on until the first goal was scored. Three times County's Ken Shaw had chances to add to the two goals he had scored in the first 90 minutes. Each time the chance went begging. The game went on and on. County's Les Cocker put the ball into the Doncaster net only for referee Baker of Crewe to disallow it for an infringement.

There were 12,730 spectators at the game and most stayed until the end. Some went home for their tea and then came back again! The heat began to take its toll. After 200 minutes, County's Rickards tried a shot in the fading light. The ball cannoned off two Rovers' defender and the goalkeeper – all three players were left laid out! Eventually after 203 minutes, the referee ended the endurance test. The two teams tossed a coin for choice of ground in the replay. Rovers won the toss and chose their own ground, where the following Wednesday, they beat County 4-0.

LOWEST

The lowest number of goals scored by Stockport County in a single Football League season is 27 in 1969-70 when the club finished bottom of the Third Division. The club's lowest points record in the Football League also occurred in 1969-70 when they gained just 23 points and were relegated.

LYTHGOE, ALF

Stockport County's greatest pre-war goal-scorer, Alf Lythgoe began his career as an amateur with Crewe Alexandra but was released for being too small. He then moved into non-League football, playing for Whitchurch, Congleton and Sandbach, where he scored a club record 55 goals. In 1931 he joined Ashton National where the following season he scored 42 goals. This feat aroused a number of local league clubs and in the summer of 1932, he signed for Stockport County.

He made his first team debut in a 2-1 defeat at Rotherham United, replacing the injured Joe Griffiths. It took the Nantwich-born forward seven matches before he scored for the club but after that, there was no holding him. He scored 19 goals in his last 14 games of that season, hitting his first hat-trick in a 3-0 win over Gateshead.

In 1933-34 he scored a record breaking 46 League goals in only 39 games and a total of 52 League and Cup goals in 44 games. He scored four goals in the defeats of Southport (Home 9-2) and Wrexham (Home 7-3) and hat-tricks against Darlington (Home 6-0), Southport (Away 4-1) and Mansfield Town (Home 3-1). Rather surprisingly, he only netted twice in the 13-0 victory against Halifax Town!

In the opening match of the 1934-35 season, he scored five goals as Southport were beaten 6-1 and netted two more hat-tricks against Gateshead (Home 5-1) and Barrow (Away 4-1) before he joined Huddersfield Town for £3,500 in October 1934.

He ended his first season at Leeds Road with the distinction of being the leading League goal-scorer both at Huddersfield with 21 goals and at County, for whom he had scored 15 goals in 10 games. Whilst with the Yorkshire club, he represented the Football League against the Irish League in Belfast. After scoring 46 goals in 79 League and Cup games, he left Huddersfield to rejoin County but arrived too late to save the club being relegated to the Third Division.

One of the club's all-time greats, he scored another 20 goals in 1938-39 to take his career record with the Edgeley Park club to 110 goals in 129 League and Cup games.

M

McCULLOCH, BILLY

The tough-tackling Scottish half-back first appeared for Stockport County during the Second World War when he was stationed with the RAF and though he was registered with the club in 1945, he did not appear in the last season of regionalised football. On the resumption of League football in 1946-47, McCulloch was made captain and over the next eight seasons made 338 League and Cup appearances, being ever-present in seasons 1946-47 and 1950-51.

He left Edgeley Park in the summer of 1954 and joined Rochdale where in four seasons at Scotland, he made 140 League appearances.

Whilst with County, the popular Scot had been carried from the Maine Road pitch with concussion after scoring the club's extra-time winner against Shrewsbury Town in a second round replay and required a serious operation. The Stockport fans didn't forget his bravery, for in 1960 when it became known that Billy McCulloch had multiple sclerosis, an appeal fund was set up to try to pay off his mortgage. A sum of £1,220 was raised, enough for the deeds of his house to be bought and handed over to him, but sadly, Billy McCulloch died the following year, aged only 39.

McGUIGAN, JIMMY

Jimmy McGuigan began his career with Hamilton Academicals before moving to Sunderland in the summer of 1947. His two seasons at Roker Park saw him play in just three First Division games before signing for County in June 1949.

He made a goal-scoring debut in a 4-0 win at Chester on the opening day of the 1949-50 season, going on to score 12 goals in 45 League and Cup games. It came as a complete surprise four games into the following season when he was allowed to leave Edgeley Park for Crewe Alexandra.

He scored 32 goals in 207 league games for the Gresty Road club before ending his playing career with Rochdale for whom he appeared in 70 games. He then returned to Crewe, first as trainer and then as the club's manager in the summer of 1960. In 1962-63 he guided the Railwaymen to promotion for the first time in their history before a year later, moving to take charge at Grimsby Town. After three years at Blundell Park he resigned, soon becoming manager of Chesterfield. Within three years, he had led the Spireites to the Fourth Division championship but then left to manage Rotherham United. In 1974-75 he led the Millmoor club to promotion from the Fourth Division and two years later, the club were deprived of promotion to the Second Division on goal average.

In November 1979, he returned to Edgeley Park, the club winning its first three games under his charge and by the end of the season, had managed to avoid having to apply for re-election. Though he was the first County manager to survive more than two seasons since Jimmy Meadows in the 1960s, he left his post in April 1982. During his time in charge, he broke the club's transfer record by paying £25,000 to Albion Rovers for Tony Coyle.

McMILLAN, SAMMY

Belfast-born Sammy McMillan signed amateur forms for Linfield but was playing for Boyland Boys Club when he was spotted by Manchester United. After working his way through the club's junior ranks, he made his first team debut for the Old Trafford club in a 3-1 defeat at Sheffield Wednesday in November 1961. He went on to score six goals in 15 games for the reds before Wrexham paid £8,000 to take him to the Racecourse Ground.

Capped twice at full international level during his time at Old Trafford, McMillan enjoyed his longest spell with the Welsh club. He scored 62 goals in 172 League and Cup games before Southend United paid £6,000 for his services in September 1967.

He never really settled at Roots Hall and two seasons later he returned to the north-west when he signed for Chester. His time at Sealand Road was hampered by injuries and because the club were short of players, he was forced to play despite a bad muscle injury. In July 1970, he joined a Stockport County side that had just been relegated to the Fourth Division. He was made captain and though County failed to gain promotion, he was the club's top-scorer with 16 goals and voted the Player of the Year. He was top scorer again in 1971-72 but a back injury forced him to quit the game, after he had netted 31 goals in 80 League and Cup appearances for the Edgeley Park side.

MANAGERS

The following is a complete list of Stockport County's full-time managers together with the inclusive dates for which they held office. Biographies of all the managers of the club are included in alphabetical order elsewhere in this A-Z.

Fred Stewart	1894-1911	Wally Galbraith	1969-1970
Harry Lewis	1911-1914	Matt Woods	1970-1971
David Ashworth	1914-1919	Brian Doyle	1972-1974
Albert Williams	1919-1924	Jimmy Meadows	1974-1975
Fred Scotchbrook	1924-1926	Roy Chapman	1975-1976
Lincoln Hyde	1926-1931	Eddie Quigley	1976-1977
Andrew Wilson	1932-1933	Alan Thompson	1977-1978
Fred Westgarth	1934-1936	Mike Summerbee	1978-1979
Bob Kelly	1936-1938	Jimmy McGuigan	1979-1982
George Hunt	1938-1939	Eric Webster	1982-1985
Bob Marshall	1939-1949	Colin Murphy	1985
Andy Beattie	1949-1952	Les Chapman	1985-1986
Dick Duckworth	1952-1956	Jimmy Melia	1986
Willie Moir	1956-1960	Colin Murphy	1986-1987
Reg Flewin	1960-1963	Asa Hartford	1987-1989
Trevor Porteous	1963-1965	Danny Bergara	1989-1995
Bert Trautmann	1965	Dave Jones	1995-1997
Eddie Quigley	1965-1966	Gary Megson	1997-
Jimmy Meadows	1966-1969		

MANCHESTER SENIOR CUP

Stockport County won the Manchester Senior Cup on four occasions. The first was in 1898 when they beat Manchester City 2-1 after County had lodged an appeal that City's outside-left Dougal was ineligible in a first match that County lost 4-0. The club retained the trophy the following season with a 2-1 final win over First Division Bury. Once again though, the club's progress was subject to controversy as after beating Ashton North End 2-1 in the semi-final, their old rivals protested about the ground and the goalposts. The match was replayed with County winning 2-0.

County had to wait until 1915 for their next success in the competition when they beat Rochdale in the final. At the end of normal time, the score was 1-1 but an exciting period of extra-time saw the Hatters run out winners 4-3.

The club last won the Manchester Senior Cup in 1923 when after defeating Bolton Wanderers and Manchester City in earlier rounds, they beat Stalybridge Celtic 2-0 in the final at Hyde Road.

MARATHON MATCHES

During the 1904-05 season when County were not members of the Football League, they beat Stalybridge Celtic 2-0 before being drawn to play Glossop in the fourth qualifying round of the FA Cup. The first game at Glossop ended 1-1 and so the replay took place at Edgeley Park. The match was abandoned in extra-time because of fading light with neither team having found the net. A FA Commission ruled that the game should be replayed at Stockport and this match was also abandoned, this time at half-time with the scored still 0-0 after a blinding snowstorm had made playing conditions nigh impossible. The tie was eventually decided at the fourth attempt with an Edwin Bardsley goal giving County a 1-0 win.

MARKSMEN – LEAGUE

Stockport County's top League goal-scorer is Jack Connor, who struck 132 League goals during six seasons at Edgeley Park. Only two players have hit more than 100 league goals for the club:

1.	Jack Connor	132
2.	Alf Lythgoe	104
3.	Kevin Francis	88
4.	Frank Newton	86
5.	Norman Rodgers	72
6.	Harry Burgess	71
7.	Joe Hill	63
8.	Brett Angell	62
9.	Joe Smith	61
10.	Jim Gannon	52
11.	Tommy Sword	52

MARKSMEN – OVERALL

Only three players have hit a century of goals for Stockport County. The club's top marksman is Jack Connor. The Century Club consists of:

1.	Jack Connor	140
2.	Kevin Francis	117
3.	Alf Lythgoe	110

MARSDEN, CHRIS

Chris Marsden began his career with Sheffield United before moving to nearby Huddersfield Town, where his career took off. He appeared in 155 first team games for the Terriers and had a short spell at Coventry City before joining Wolverhampton Wanderers for £250,000 in January 1994. He never really settled at Molineux and in November of that year he moved to Notts County for the same transfer fee. At Meadow Lane he was hampered by injuries and after just 12 games for the Magpies, he joined Stockport County on loan, the move becoming permanent in January 1996.

He made his debut in a 4-3 defeat at Burnley but soon made himself a big Edgeley Park favourite with a number of 'Man of the Match' awards. He masterminded the club's late season push for promotion, making the £70,000 transfer fee look a real bargain.

In 1996-97, the astute and very competitive player made a big contribution to the club reaching the League Cup semi-finals and winning promotion to the First Division.

MARSHALL, BOBBY

Bobby Marshall was a brilliant ball-playing inside-forward who began his league career with Sunderland. He went on to score 71 goals in 205 appearances for the then Roker Park club before joining Manchester City in March 1928. By the end of his first season he had helped the Maine Road club win the Second Division championship. Five years later he was a member of the City side beaten 3-0 by Everton in the FA Cup Final but was back in 1934 as City beat Portsmouth 2-1. After being converted to centre-half, Marshall won a League Championship medal and during his Maine Road career, scored 80 goals in 355 appearances.

He was appointed County's manager in March 1939, but within six months of taking charge at Edgeley Park, war broke out and the Football League was suspended. He left for Reading to join the army's physical training staff and only returned to manage County in 1945. On the resumption of League football in 1946-47 he led the club to fourth place in the Third Division (North). The following season, County finished in 17th place, their worst-ever position in the Third Division (North). They improved to finish eighth in 1948-49 but in February of that season, Marshall left to manage Chesterfield.

Under him, the Spireites finished sixth but two years later they were relegated and he left football management for good.

MASSEY, STEVE

Born in Denton, Steve Massey played schoolboy representative football and ran in the Lancashire Schools cross-country championships before signing apprentice forms for Stockport County.

He made his first team debut at the age of 16, coming on as a substitute for Norman Lloyd in the 2-1 win over Darlington and scoring the

Steve Massey

winning goal. After being rewarded with a full-time contract, Massey went on to appear in 114 League and Cup games for the Edgeley Park club, scoring 24 goals, many of which were important strikes.

He left County at the end of the 1977-78 season to sign for Bournemouth but left Dean Court before the Cherries won promotion. After a brief spell with Peterborough United he joined Northampton Town, where he scored 26 goals in 60 league games. Then he joined Hull City who won promotion from the Third Division but before he could sample Second Division football, he was released and joined Cambridge United. A year later he joined his seventh and final League club, Wrexham, ending his career with a total of 97 goals in 392 league appearances.

MEADOWS, JIMMY

Bolton-born Jimmy Meadows' playing career began with the local YMCA before he made his Football League debut with Southport. In March 1951, he moved to Manchester City, winning an England cap in the 7-2 win over Scotland in April 1955. Unfortunately, he had to retire from playing at the age of 26 after a bad knee injury received in the FA Cup Final of 1956.

He remained on the training staff at Maine Road for a number of years before replacing Billy Newton as the Edgeley Park club's trainer. Promoted to manager in October 1966, his first season saw County win the Fourth Division championship. Two seasons in the Third Division followed but then he was sacked after fielding a player against Chairman Victor Bernard's instructions!

After spells on the staff of Bury and Blackpool, he returned to his home-town club in January 1971, to become the Wanderers' team manager. In charge for only 11 weeks at Burnden Park, he left with the team bottom of the Second Division. In 1972-73 he took Southport to the Fourth Division championship before returning to County in May 1974. The following season saw the club just escape the re-election zone on the final day of the season, but in August 1975, Meadows was sacked. He then had a spell as caretaker manager of Blackpool, later becoming assistant-manager of the Kuwait Sporting Club before coaching in Sweden.

MEGSON, GARY

The son of the former Sheffield Wednesday captain, Don Megson, he made his league debut for Plymouth Argyle and spent two seasons with the Home Park club before joining Everton for £250,000, a figure that broke Argyle's transfer record. In August 1981, Jack Charlton brought Megson to Hillsborough and in 1983-84 he was ever-present as the Owls won promotion to the First Division. He later joined Nottingham Forest but after three months without a game he left to play for Newcastle United, who were then managed by Jack Charlton. When Charlton left St James' Park, Megson was left in the cold and jumped at the chance of a return to Sheffield Wednesday. He stayed three years in his second spell at Hillsborough before being allowed to join Manchester City where he marked his debut with the only goal of the game against Oldham Athletic. He helped the club win promotion before being given a free transfer and joining Norwich city. Caretaker-manager for the last five games of the 1994-95 season, he played on a non-contract basis for Lincoln and Shrewsbury before being appointed first team coach at Bradford City. After a spell in charge at Blackpool, he was appointed manager at Stockport County in July 1997, and in his first season in charge at Edgeley Park he led the Hatters to eighth place in the First Division, the club's highest ever Football League placing.

Gary Megson

MELIA, JIMMY

Capped at schoolboy and youth level, Jimmy Melia began his career with Liverpool, where he eventually won a full England cap in 1963 and gained a second cap later that year, as England beat Switzerland 8-1 in Basle with Melia scoring one of the goals. He had scored 78 goals in 287 games for the Reds when he lost his place and was transferred to Wolverhampton Wanderers for £55,000.

Eight months later, he was on his way to Southampton, where his vast experience helped the Saints avoid relegation during their first season in the top flight. He later played for Aldershot before ending his playing career with Crewe Alexandra.

A flamboyant manager, Melia took Aldershot to the fourth round of the 1969-70 FA Cup competition but two seasons later, with the Shots near the foot of the table, he was sacked. He then took charge at Crewe but the Gresty Road club had to seek re-election twice during his term of office and he left to manage Southport. He lasted only three months at Haig Avenue before joining Brighton who reached the FA Cup Final in his spell there. Melia resigned when Chris Cattlin was appointed coach and went to manage Portuguese side Beleneses.

In July 1986, he re-

Jimmy Melia

turned to England to manage Stockport County but after only one win in the first 14 games of the 1986-87 season, Melia was dismissed after less than four months in charge.

MILLER, DAVID

The son of the legendary Burnley player, Brian Miller, who was in fact the Turf Moor club's manager when David made his break-through into League football with his home-town club on New Year's Day 1983. The first-ever son of a former Claret to appear in the league side he went on to appear in 41 first team games before being released in May 1985.

After a season at Tranmere, he joined Colne Dynamoes, but then

David Miller

suddenly he was back in league football, signing for Fourth Division Preston in December 1986.

At the end of his first season he helped North End to promotion and then after a short loan spell back at Turf moor joined Carlisle in September 1989. At Brunton Park, Miller enjoyed regular first team football where his consistency at full-back and in midfield even-tually attracted Stockport County, who paid £25,000 for his services in March 1992.

In two seasons as a regu-lar at Edgeley Park, Miller appeared in the play-offs twice, the second against his former club Burnley in May 1994. The experi-enced and reliable defender went on to appear in 106 first team games for County before joining Wigan Athletic in October 1994. At Springfield Park he found it difficult to break into the club's central defence and was released in the summer of 1996. Having played all his football in the north-west, Miller made 436 appearances for his seven clubs.

MOIR, WILLIE

Willie Moir hailed from Bucksburn, Aberdeenshire and began his career with the 25th Old Boys' FC before joining Bucksburn Juniors. During the Second World War he joined the RAF and was posted to a camp at Kirkham, where he was spotted by Bolton Wanderers scout, Bob Jackson. He soon signed professional forms for the Trotters but 'guested' for both Aberdeen and Dundee before playing for the Wanderers in the North v South Cup Final in 1945. In 1948-49 he topped the First Division scoring charts with 25 goals, including all the goals in a 4-2 win at Aston Villa.

Moir's only Scottish appearance came against England in Glasgow in April 1950, and three years later he captained Bolton in the 'Matthews Final' when Blackpool beat a depleted Wanderers' side 4-3.

In September 1955, after 12 years at Burnden Park, he joined Stockport County and in June the following year, was appointed player-manager. In his first season in charge, County finished fifth and then in 1957-58, ninth. His third season at the club saw County manage to 'qualify' for the newly formed Third Division but this was followed by relegation to the Fourth Division. After the club failed to win immediate promotion in 1959-60, Moir was sacked.

In March 1961, he joined Lancashire Combination side Nelson as manager before returning to Bolton, where he helped out on the commercial side until his death in 1988.

MORAN, EDDIE

Eddie Moran was a Scotland Schoolboy international who impressed both Manchester United and Leicester City but it was the Filbert Street club for whom he signed in September 1947. He made his debut for Leicester in a highly physical game against Grimsby Town, Moran being one of only three full fit City players at the end of the game! However, despite some impressive performances for the reserves, he only made eight first team appearances in two years at the club and after a disagreement with Leicester manager Norman Bullock, he returned home to Scotland.

Having asked for a transfer, Moran was amazed to find the club asking £15,000 for him and made three requests to the Football League to get the fee reduced. Though a number of clubs showed an interest in him, it was Stockport County who persuaded him to join them for a club record fee of £5,000. He partnered Jack Connor on his debut in a 1-0 win at Hartlepool United on 27th October 1951. His one and only hat-trick for the club came the following season when County beat Bradford City 6-1 at Edgeley Park. Though he wasn't a prolific scorer – netting 47 times in 117 games for County – he scored in five consecutive matches at the end of the 1955-56 season, as well as netting goals in the opening two matches of the following campaign.

In February 1957, he joined Rochdale and later had a spell with Crewe Alexandra before a knee ligament injury ended his career at the age of 27.

MOST GOALS IN A SEASON

When Stockport County finished third in the Third Division (North) in 1933-34 they scored 115 goals in 42 matches. It was during this season that they beat Halifax Town 13-0, Southport 9-2 and Wrexham 7-3. Top-scorer was Alf Lythgoe with 46 goals in 39 games including four in each of the victories over Southport and Wrexham.

MOST MATCHES

Stockport County played their most number of matches, 67, in the 1996-97 season. This comprised 46 League games, four FA Cup games, 11 Football League Cup games and six games in the Autowindscreen Shield.

MULHEARN, KEN

Though he played right-half during his early schooldays, Ken Mulhearn's height was enough to persuade him to move to goalkeeper. This was the position in which he played for Liverpool and Lancashire Boys. He also forced his way into the England Boys squad but was kept out of the side by Alan Ogley, who in 1967, was part of the exchange deal that took Mulhearn to Manchester City.

It was while playing for Liverpool Boys, that Mulhearn was spotted by Everton. Having spent three seasons in the reserves, his opportunities for first team football became even more limited when the Toffees signed Gordon West from Blackpool for £27,000, a record fee for a goalkeeper. After turning down a move to Torquay United he signed for County in August 1964.

Replacing Graham Beighton he made his debut in a 2-0 defeat at Oxford United on 7th October 1964 and went on to appear in 117 League and Cup games, including winning a Fourth Division championship medal in 1966-67. After just five games of the following season, Manchester City offered £25,000 plus Alan Ogley to take Mulhearn to Maine Road.

He made his City debut in the Manchester derby, United winning 2-1 with Bobby Charlton scoring both goals. He then kept his place for the next 43 games before cartilage problems forced him out of the game for twelve months. However, during that 1967-68 season, City won the League Championship giving Mulhearn Fourth and First Division championship medals in consecutive campaigns. Though he played a few games in 1969-70 when City won the European Cup Winners' Cup, he was unable to regain his place and so in March 1971, he joined Shrewsbury Town.

He spent ten injury-free seasons at Gay Meadow, appearing in 370 league games. Voted the club's 'Player of the Year' on three occasions he also won a Third Division championship and Welsh Cup winners' medal.

In the summer of 1980 he signed for Crewe Alexandra, where he played the last of his 608 league games.

MURPHY, COLIN

Colin Murphy never played League football but enjoyed a career as a much respected coach and manager. After a year coaching at Charlton Athletic he took charge of Nottingham Forest's youth team before following Dave Mackay to Derby County as first team coach. Following Mackay's departure in November 1976, Murphy took over as manager but had a tough time at the Baseball Ground. He was nearly replaced by Brian Clough and Peter Taylor in February 1977, but they turned down the offer of a return to Derby. Eventually he was dismissed but within a month he had become assistant to Jimmy Sirrel at Notts County In November 1978, he became manager at Lincoln City and in 1980-81 led them to promotion from the Fourth Division.

Murphy became Stockport County manager in August 1985, but after just four games in charge, he received a good offer to coach in Saudi Arabia and left Edgeley Park. In October 1986, following Jimmy Melia's sacking, Murphy was persuaded to return to the club. County's future looked bleak, for in March 1987, they were bottom of the Fourth Division and facing automatic relegation from the Football League. Six wins in the next nine games took them to 19th but at the end of the season, Murphy left to rejoin Lincoln who had lost their League status. After leading the Imps back as champions of the Conference, he coached at Leicester City and Luton Town before managing Southend United. However, with the Roots Hall club looking like relegation candidates he lost his job to Barry Fry.

MURRAY, BOB

Wing-half Bob Murray's early football was played with Inverurie Locos where he was learning a trade on the railways, but in November 1951, County manager Andy Beattie persuaded the 19-year-old Scotsman to join the Edgeley Park club. He continued to play football as he completed his National Service and made his debut in a 1-1 draw at home to Halifax Town in September 1952.

Between 28th August 1954 and 14th February 1959, Murray played in 213 consecutive League matches and in fact, missed just four matches in those five seasons. Made captain of County during this period, the tough-tackling Murray never missed a FA Cup tie during his 11 seasons at Edgeley Park. He went on to appear in 495 League and Cup games for the Hatters and his total of 465 League games was a club record until broken by Andy Thorpe in 1991. Not a prolific goal-scorer, both the first and last of his 32 goals for the club came in matches against York City at Edgeley Park – 1-1 in 1952-53 and 2-1 in 1961-62.

Released at the end of the 1962-63 season he moved into non-League football with Bangor City before ending his playing career with Ashton United.

MUTCH, ANDY

Liverpool-born forward Andy Mutch began his career with Southport before joining Wolverhampton Wanderers in February 1986. Forming a deadly scoring partnership with Steve Bull, he helped the club win the Fourth and Third Division championships in successive seasons and in seven years at Molineux scored 105 goals in 338 first team games.

Surprisingly allowed to join Swindon Town for £250,000 in the summer of 1993 he had netted 12 goals in 64 games when just five

Andy Mutch

games into the 1995-96 season he was loaned to Wigan Athletic, where he scored on his debut in a 1-1 home draw against Preston North End. After the clubs had failed to agree terms, Mutch returned to the County Ground where he then spent several months in the wilderness.

Eventually in March 1996, Mutch accepted a move to Stockport County and soon burst into action with a hat-trick in the important 4-2 home win over promotion rivals Oxford United. Although County just failed to reach the First Division, there was no doubting the wisdom of the move, for in 1996-97 he played an important role in the club winning promotion and reaching the semi-finals of the League Cup, where he scored an 83rd minute winner in the 2-1 victory at Southampton.

N

NEUTRAL GROUNDS

Stockport have had to replay on a neutral ground during the FA Cup competition a number of times:

Date	Opponents	Venue	FA Cup	Score
28.11.1910	Rochdale	Boundary Park	Round 1	0-1
22.12.1947	Shrewsbury	Town Maine Road	Round 2	3-2
03.12.1951	Gateshead	Hillsborough	Round 1	1-2
05.12.1966	Darlington	Elland Road	Round 2	2-4

The club have also had to replay on a neutral ground on two occasions in the Football League Cup:

28.08.1972	Bradford City	Burnden Park	Round 1	2-0
30.08.1976	Workington	Deepdale	Round 1	2-0

County have also played on a neutral ground during the Third Division (North) Challenge Cup Finals of 1934 and 1935 when they lost 4-3 to Darlington at Old Trafford in 1934 and beat Walsall 2-0 at Maine Road in 1935. All the club's appearances at Wembley in the play-offs and the final of the Autoglass Trophy also qualify for inclusion.

NEWTON, FRANK

After leaving the army, Frank Newton joined non-League Ashton United, from where he joined County in January 1928. After making his debut in a 4-1 defeat at Ashington two months later, he found that for the next season or so, his opportunities were limited by the presence of Harry Burgess and Joe Smith, though he did score 16 goals in 19 league games in 1928-29. Before the start of the following season, Burgess had joined Sheffield Wednesday and Joe Smith had retired, so it was Newton who partnered new signing Andy Lincoln. He went on to score 36 goals in 35 league appearances including five goals in a 6-1 win over Nelson, four in a 6-1 defeat of Rotherham United and all three in a 3-0 victory over Doncaster Rovers. Remarkably in early January after scoring 21 goals in the first 22 matches of the season he was dropped!

In 1930-31, 'Bonzo' Newton as he was known scored 34 goals in 39 league games including hat-tricks against Gateshead (Home 3-1) and Lincoln City (home 4-2). After scoring 93 goals in only 101 League and Cup games, Newton left Edgeley Park but surprisingly joined another Third Division team in Fulham. After netting 74 goals in 75 games for the Cottagers he left to spend a season with Reading, where he found the net 29 times in 32 games. He then rejoined Fulham but within two months of his return, his career was over as he broke a leg in a friendly match. Newton was only 32 and had scored a remarkable 192 goals in 209 League appearances for his three clubs.

NICKNAMES

Because Stockport was a Hat making town, it was only natural that when County were looking for a nickname, the idea of 'The Hatters' was thought the only one suitable. However, in recent years, the term 'Hatters' has rarely been used and supporters have always it seems preferred 'County' as the club nickname. Many players in the club's history have been fondly known by their nicknames. They include:

Frank Newton, 1928-1933: 'Bonzo'

Jack Bowles, 1938-1953: 'Tiger'

Gordon Wilmott, 1948-1959: 'The Bull'

Kevin Francis, 1991-1995: 'Bigman'

NON-LEAGUE

'Non-League' is the shorthand term for clubs which are not members of the Football League. The club's record against non-League opposition in the FA Cup since the Second World War is as follows:

Date	Opponents	FA Cup	Venue	Score
26.11.1949	Billingham	Round 1	Home	3-0
22.11.1952	North Shields	Round 1	Away	6-2
10.01.1953	Walthamstow Ave	Round 3	Away	1-2
09.01.1954	Headington United	Round 3	Home	0-0
14.01.1954	Headington United	Round 3R	Away	0-1
17.11.1956	New Brighton	Round 1	Away	3-3
21.11.1956	New Brighton	Round 1R	Home	2-3
06.12.1958	Blyth Spartans	Round 2	Away	4-3
14.11.1959	West Auckland	Round 1	Away	6-2
26.11.1960	Bishop Auckland	Round 2	Home	2-0
14.11.1964	Wigan Athletic	Round 1	Home	2-1
09.12.1967	Macclesfield	Round 1	Home	1-1
13.12.1967	Macclesfield	Round 1R	Away	1-2
15.11.1969	Mossley	Round 1	Home	1-1
17.11.1969	Mossley	Round 1R	Away	1-0
21.11.1970	Grantham	Round 1	Away	1-2
11.12.1971	Blyth Spartans	Round 2	Away	0-1
23.11.1974	Stafford Rangers	Round 1	Home	0-0
26.11.1974	Stafford Rangers	Round 1R	Away	0-1
25.11.1978	Morecambe	Round 1	Home	5-1
21.11.1981	Mossley	Round 1	Home	3-1
19.11.1983	Telford United	Round 1	Away	0-3
16.11.1985	Telford United	Round 1	Home	0-1
15.11.1986	Caernarfon Town	Round 1	Away	0-1
14.11.1987	Telford United	Round 1	Away	1-1
17.11.1987	Telford United	Round 1R	Home	2-0
05.12.1992	Macclesfield	Round 2	Away	2-0
02.12.1995	Blyth Spartans	Round 2	Home	2-0

NORTHERN SECTION CUP

The inaugural Northern Section Cup took place in 1933-34 when County fought their way through to the final, beating Rochdale (Away 4-2), Accrington Stanley (Home 1-0) and Mansfield Town (Home 4-0). In the final they met Darlington at Old Trafford. County were leading 3-2 with just two minutes remaining but saw the trophy snatched from their grasp by two late goals from the Quakers.

In 1934-35 County reached the final again, beating Accrington Stanley (Away 2-1), Halifax Town (Home 3-1 after a goal-less draw at The Shay), Rochdale (Home 3-0) and Hartlepool United (Home 6-2). Their opponents in the final at Maine Road were Walsall. This time County made no mistake, winning 2-0 with a goal from Billy McNaughton and an own goal by Saddlers' Bennett.

In 1935-36, County went out in the first round, losing 2-0 at Barrow and 4-0 in the second round at Port Vale the following season. Afterwards the club did not enter the competition as it was restricted to those Division Three (North) clubs who had not reached the third round of the FA Cup.

OGLEY, ALAN

One of the bravest and most agile goalkeepers ever to play for Stockport County, Alan Ogley was a more than useful all-round sportsman, playing both football and cricket for England Schoolboys to become the first double international at that level.

At the age of 15 he joined the ground staff at Barnsley but in the summer of 1963, after appearing in just nine games for his hometown team, he joined Manchester City. In four seasons at Maine Road, he made 57 League and Cup appearances before he was used as part-exchange in the deal which took Ken Mulhearn in the opposite direction.

He made his debut for County in a 2-1 defeat at Tranmere Rovers in September 1967, and though he suffered a bad injury in his first season at Edgeley Park he went on to appear in 269 games for the club and was ever-present in seasons 1969-70 and 1972-73 when he was voted the club's Player of the Year.

In the summer of 1975 he moved to Darlington but after just one season with the Quakers he retired from League football. One of the most popular of County players, only Jack 'Tiger' Bowles has made more appearances as a goalkeeper for the Edgeley Park club.

OLDEST PLAYER

The oldest player to line-up in a Stockport County first team is Alec Herd. He was 40 years 47 days old when he played his last game for the club against Crewe Alexandra (Home 4-2) in a Third Division (North) game on Christmas Day 1951.

OLD TRAFFORD

On 7th May 1921, a record attendance was set when a crowd of just 13 paid to watch Stockport County play Leicester City in a Second Division match. Edgeley Park had been closed by the Football Association and so the game was played at Old Trafford. The attendance is somewhat misleading in that the game was watched by a lot more who had stayed on after the Manchester United v Derby County game. Over 10,000 remained inside the ground to watch the game, which was goal-less, for free!

OLIVER, ALAN

Outside-left Alan Oliver could always be relied upon for his consistency. He joined Stockport County from Derby County in August 1950, and made his debut in a 3-1 home win over Bradford City on the opening day of the 1950-51 season. Though never a prolific scorer, he did find the net 32 times in 151 League and Cup games for County in four seasons at Edgeley Park, with a best of 14 in 1951-52. Oliver was frequently the provider of crosses from which Andy Black and Jack Connor scored the majority of their goals.

In the summer of 1954 he joined Gateshead and had a similar record there, netting 36 goals in 146 League appearances.

OVERSEAS PLAYERS

Among the overseas players to represent Stockport County are Joel Cantona, a Frenchman signed from Ujpest Dozsa. He made three substitute appearances in 1993-94 but was not retained at the end of the season.

Two Portuguese players to represent County in 1996-97 were Luis Caveco from Estoril and Manuel Kiko from Belenenses, the former scoring five goals in 27 league games as the club ended the season as runners-up to Bury in the Second Division. At the beginning of the 1997-98 campaign, Vas Kaligeracos made four League and Cup appearances.

Other players with foreign-sounding surnames include Michael Czuczman, William Froehlich, Peter Olynik, George Oghani and Stephen Uzelac – all born in the British Isles!

P

PARK, TERRY

One of the most gifted midfielders ever to play for the club, Terry Park began his career with Wolverhampton Wanderers but after failing to make the first team, joined Blackpool as a non-contract player. He improved in the Bloomfield Road club's reserve side who were managed by Eddie Quigley but they had no money to buy him. When Quigley returned to take charge at Edgeley Park for a second time in May 1976, he signed Park and the Liverpool-born player made his first team debut as a substitute in a 2-0 home win over Brentford on 23rd August 1976. However, he had only played in five League and Cup games when he was forced to undergo a cartilage operation and missed the rest of the season.

He returned to first team football in August 1977, and over the next two and a half seasons hardly missed a game before he and fellow County player Ken Fogarty joined Fort Lauderdale in the United States for a combined fee of £100,000. After playing alongside George Best and Gerd Muller he signed for Minnesota Kicks for £50,000.

The popular Scouser returned to Edgeley Park for a second spell in

March 1981, and took his club record to 24 goals in 181 games before a disagreement with club officials forced him to leave.

Though County still held the player's registration, he had a loan spell with Manchester City before joining Bury in the summer of 1983. After one injury-hit season with the Gigg Lane club, he gave up professional football to run a post office with his wife.

PATERSON, ALEX

After playing wartime football with Alloa Athletic, Alex Paterson joined New Brighton and in 70 games for the Rakers, scored ten goals, mainly from the inside-forward position. In March 1948, he joined County as part of the exchange deal which took Albert Earl to New Brighton.

He made his debut for County in a 1-1 draw at Gateshead and over the next five seasons gave consistent performances in the left-half position. In 1949-50 he appeared in all the club's 48 League and Cup matches as County reached the fifth round before losing 2-1 at home to Liverpool.

Eventually losing his place to Bob Murray, Paterson who had made 171 League and Cup appearances for County, joined Barrow and later Halifax Town but failed to make a first team appearance at either club.

PENALTIES

The most successful penalty-taker in the club's history is Tommy Sword who netted 25 of his 55 goals from the penalty-spot – 24 in the Football League and one that helped give County a 2-1 League Cup win against Sunderland at Roker Park on 3rd September 1980.

During the 1928-29 season when County were pushing for promotion to the Second Division they entertained Cheshire rivals Crewe Alexandra on Good Friday. The loss of a point in a 2-2 draw was bad enough but the club missed two penalties, the first by Frank Hudspeth and the second by Harry Burgess who was on a hat-trick!

Crewe were the club that ended County's record-breaking home run the following season when they won 3-2 at Edgeley Park. Frank

Newton missed a penalty which would also have given him a hat-trick and of course preserved the club's record.

When County lost 3-0 at Lincoln City on 16th September 1935, all three of the Sincil Bank club's goals came from penalties!

County goalkeeper Jack Bowles saved two penalties in the match against York City on 15th January 1949, from the Minstermen's captain and expert penalty-taker Harry Brigham. Unfortunately, County lost 4-0. The Stockport 'keeper then went on to repeat the feat in the same fixture the following season which County drew 1-1.

PITCH

The Edgeley Park pitch measures 111 yards x 72 yards.

PLASTIC

There have been four Football League clubs that replaced their normal grass playing pitches with artificial surfaces at one stage or another. Queen's Park Rangers were the first in 1981, but the Loftus Road plastic was discarded in 1988 in favour of a return to turf. Luton Town (1985), Oldham Athletic (1985) and Preston North End (1986) followed.

County have only played on the Deepdale plastic and on their first visit on 17 March 1987, lost 3-0. The club's next met on the artificial surface on Boxing Day 1991 when despite being helped by an own goal from a North End defender, County still lost 3-2. The club's last met on the plastic on 20th March 1993, when two goals from Peter Duffield helped County to a 3-2 success.

PLAYER POWER

During the 1901-02 season, Stockport County players, fed up with not being paid, declared themselves independent, picked their own team and shared the gate money among themselves. Player power worked as the team just retained its Second Division status.

PLAY-OFFS

Stockport County have been involved in the play-offs at the end of the season on four occasions.

The first was in 1989-90 when the club finished fourth in Division Four and met Chesterfield in the play-off semi-final. A disastrous first-leg at Saltergate, where the Spireites won 4-0 with Calvin Palmer grabbing a hat-trick, put paid to any hopes of County reaching the Wembley final. Three days later, County went down 2-0 at Edgeley Park in the second leg.

After winning promotion to the Third Division in 1990-91, County reached the play-offs a second time after finishing fifth in Division Three. Meeting fellow Autoglass finalists Stoke City in the semi-final, County won the Edgeley Park encounter with a Peter Ward free-kick finding its way into Sinclair's top left-hand corner of his goal. At the

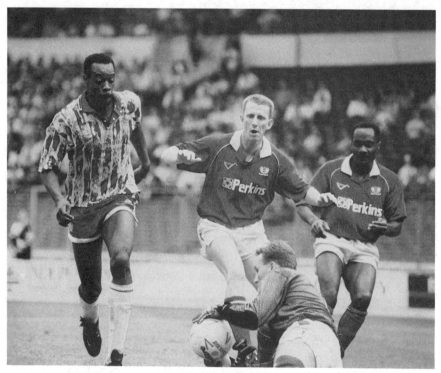

Action from the 1992 Play-Off

1994 Play-Off v. Burnley

Victoria Ground, Chris Beaumont scored in the first minute to give County a two-goal cushion and though Mark Stein pulled a late goal back for the Potters, it wasn't enough and County were in the play-off final against Peterborough United. A crowd of 35,087 were inside Wembley Stadium to see Peterborough take the lead in controversial circumstances when Ken Charlery's header was allowed to stand, although David Frain wasn't convinced that the whole of the ball had crossed the line. County fought hard for the equaliser which eventually came from Kevin Francis with just three minutes left. Unbelievably the game was in its last minute when Charlery lobbed Neil Edwards for his and Peterborough's second goal.

County reached the play-offs for a third time the following season after ending the campaign in sixth place in the 'new' Second Division. In the first play-off semi-final at Edgeley Park, County drew 1-1 with Port Vale with Jim Gannon netting from the spot for the Hatters. Despite Kevin Francis being suspended for the return leg, County did have enough chances to cause an upset but lost 1-0 to a Martin Foyle goal five minutes from time.

The club reached the play-offs again in 1993-94 and after a great defensive display in the first leg at Bootham Crescent, held York City to a goal-less draw. The second leg at Edgeley Park was also a close contest, it taking a superb Chris Beaumont goal to separate the teams. County faced Burnley in the Wembley final and took the lead after just two minutes when Chris Beaumont scored with a diving header from David Frain's free-kick. Mike Wallace, County's defender was sent-off after 13 minutes and a quarter-of-an-hour later, David Eyres equalised for the Clarets. County's goal-scorer Chris Beaumont was sent-off after 61 minutes to leave the Edgeley Park club with nine men. Four minutes later, Gary Parkinson scored Burnley's second and what turned out to be winning goal, whilst Adrian Heath was in an offside position!

POINTS

Under the three points for a win system which was introduced in 1981-82, Stockport County's best points tally was the 85 points in 1993-94 when the club finished fourth in the Second Division. However, the club's best points haul under the old two points for a win system was 64 points in 1966-67 when they won the Fourth Division championship. County's worst record under either system was the meagre 23 points secured in 1969-70 when the club finished bottom of the Third Division and were relegated.

PORTEOUS, TREVOR

Though he was dismissed by Stockport County three times, leaving of his own accord more than once and undergoing major heart surgery, Trevor Porteous gave the club great service over a 40-year association.

He began his playing career with his home-town club Hull City and in five and a half years with the Boothferry Park club, made 61 appearances. However, almost two years were lost when he was called up for National Service with the Army.

He signed for Stockport County for a fee of £1,500 in the summer of 1956, making his debut in a 1-0 win at Southport. Over the next nine seasons he played in 364 games for County, his final two years as player-manager.

With little back-room staff and no money, Porteous worked miracles, helping County gain a 1-1 draw at Liverpool in the FA Cup of 1964-65 before filling Edgeley Park with a crowd of 24,080 in the replay. In October 1965, having guided the club to a 7-1 win against Bradford City, their highest-ever victory at the Valley Parade, he was sacked following a disagreement with club chairman Vic Bernard. He had just become the first County player to secure a testimonial of over £1,000 when First Division Stoke City visited Edgeley Park.

He then became assistant-manager to Ernie Tagg at Crewe Alexandra but within 12 months was back at Edgeley Park in a similar capacity in support of County's new manager Jimmy Meadows. After two successful seasons in the Third Division, he was sacked again, this time following a 4-1 home defeat by Fulham.

His services were required again a few months later when he was asked to run 'The County Club'. This he did for three years before leaving to enter a variety of business ventures.

He was back at Edgeley Park again in 1975, this time as physiotherapist, but six managers and seven years later, he left to work for Stockport Social Services. Willing to do anything to further the cause of Stockport County, he returned to the club in 1987 as the Hatters'

Youth Development Officer. It took major heart by-pass surgery in 1990 to sever his official ties with the club but thankfully the operation was a success.

POSTPONED

In January 1910, County's league game against Leeds City at Leeds was called off at the last minute due to the severe frost and heavy snow. The match referee who made that decision was none other than Harry Lewis who some 18 months later became manager at Edgeley Park. When the game was eventually played on 15th March, County won 2-0 with goals from Whitehouse and Kelly.

PREECE, ANDY

After beginning his football career with Worcester City, Andy Preece joined his home-town club Evesham United. After spending two seasons with them and spending his summers playing cricket for Worcestershire Second XI, he went to Australia for six months on a cricket scholarship. On his return to these shores, he rejoined Evesham but was playing as a non-contract player for Northampton Town. Things didn't work out for him at the County Ground and after loan spells with a number of non-League clubs, he returned to Worcester City.

Eventually in March 1990, he returned to League football when Wrexham paid £4,000 to take him to the Racecourse Ground. He had scored 11 goals in 63 games when County manager Danny Bergara paid £15,000 for his services.

He made his debut as a substitute at Preston North End on Boxing Day 1991 and ended the season with 13 goals in 25 league games, including a hat-trick in a 3-1 win at Darlington. Though he was cup tied for the club's first Wembley appearance in the 1992 Autoglass Trophy final, he returned eight days later in the play-offs, supplying the cross for Kevin Francis to equalise against Peterborough United.

Preece formed a formidable striking partnership with Kevin Francis and in 1993-94 he scored 23 goals in 47 League and Cup games including hat-tricks against Swansea City (Home 4-0) and Brighton and Hove Albion (Home 3-0).

Andy Preece

His goal-scoring achievements, 54 goals in 121 games for County led to him joining Crystal Palace for a club record fee of £350,000 in June 1994.

Failing to make much of an impact at Selhurst Park, he returned to the north-west a year later, signing for Blackpool for £200,000. He ended his first season at Bloomfield Road as the club's top scorer and continues to score for the Seasiders on a regular basis.

PRICE, JOHNNY

Diminutive winger Johnny Price was spotted by Burnley playing for Hordern Colliery Welfare. He soon made a big impression at Turf Moor and was a key member of the Clarets' Central League championship side of 1962-63. He made his first team debut at West Ham in October 1963, but was restricted to just 21 games over two seasons and in May 1965, he joined Stockport County for £4,000.

The Hatters had just endured the trauma of finishing rock bottom of the Football League and successfully applied for re-election. The only way was up and Price immediately formed a successful partnership with Len Allchurch on the other flank, both wingers supplying quality crosses into the middle.

At the end of his first season at Edgeley Park, Price was voted the club's Player of the Year and in 1966-67 he was a major influence as County won the Fourth Division championship in style. He went on to appear in 274 League and Cup games before moving on in 1971 to Blackburn Rovers but returned to Stockport less than three years later. In his second spell at Edgeley Park, Price was unable to weave enough of the magic of his former stint with the club and retired in 1976 after appearing in a total of 345 first team games for the club.

At 5ft 3ins, Price was one of the smallest players to appear in British football during the post-war era. Sadly, after a long illness he passed away in 1995 at the age of only 51.

PROGRAMMES

Match programmes have changed radically over the years, but local companies continue to support Stockport County. Some examples of programmes are shown on the next few pages.

STOCKPORT COUNTY

v.

Rochdale

Monday, 9th
November, 1964

Kick-off 7-30p.m.

**FOOTBALL LEAGUE
DIVISION FOUR**

Nº 1994

Official Programme 6d

TOMMY SWORD
TESTIMONIAL

"A celebration of his loyalty and service at Edgeley Park"

PRE-SEASON FRIENDLY IN AID OF THE TOMMY SWORD TESTIMONIAL FUND

STOCKPORT COUNTY
VERSES
MANCHESTER CITY

Wednesday, 17th August, 1988.   Kick-off 7.30 p.m.

Souvenir Programme: £1.00

PROMOTION

Stockport County have been promoted on five occasions. They were first promoted as champions of the Third Division (North) in 1921-22 when they won 24 of their 38 matches and finished six points ahead of second placed Darlington.

They won promotion a second time in 1936-37 when they again won the championship of the Third Division (North) ending the season with 60 points, three ahead of runners-up, Lincoln City.

County's third experience of promotion came in 1966-67 when they won 26 of their 46 matches to win the Fourth Division championship. The trophy was presented at Edgeley Park prior to the final game of the season against Lincoln City which County lost 5-4!

They were promoted again in 1990-91 when they finished the season as runners-up to Darlington in the Fourth Division.

County last experienced promotion in 1996-97 when despite playing an extra 21 games on top of their league campaign, they finished as runners-up, just two points adrift of champions, Bury.

Q

QUICKEST GOAL

On Christmas Day 1956, County beat Accrington Stanley 2-1 in front of an Edgeley Park crowd of 8,902. Ray Drake's opening goal was timed as being after seven seconds of the game by referee Arthur Ellis and is widely accepted as the club's fastest goal ever.

QUIGLEY, EDDIE

In December 1949, Eddie Quigley became the most expensive footballer in Britain when he joined Preston North End from Sheffield Wednesday for £26,000. After two years at Deepdale he moved to Blackburn Rovers where under Johnny Carey's attacking philosophy, Quigley's goal-scoring flourished, his long-range shooting having both accuracy and power.

As a player, his movements were totally deceptive, for his speed of thought and precise passing made him a constant threat to the opposition defences. He was capable of playing both inside or centre-forward though he preferred to play much deeper than most of his contemporaries.

On leaving Ewood Park in the summer of 1956, he returned to his home-town club Bury, before entering non-League football as manager of Mossley. After returning to Gigg Lane as coach he took charge at Stockport County in October 1965.

He put together a side that became Fourth Division champions only months after he had left to become assistant-manager at Blackburn Rovers. A master tactician, he soon began to show his influence on Jack Marshall's team and following Marshall's resignation in February 1967, Quigley was appointed caretaker-manager, a position that became permanent some two months later. He lost his job when Rovers were relegated to the Third Division.

In May 1976, he returned to Edgeley Park and after the club won five of their first six games, it looked as though he would repeat his success of his first spell with the club, especially when they occupied third place at the turn of the year. Unfortunately, County hit a bad patch and plummeted down the table with the result that Quigley was sacked before the season finished.

He found employment with Blackburn Rovers a third time in 1979 when Howard Kendall appointed him chief scout, a position he held until Kendall left in 1981.

Mick Quinn

QUINN, MICK

An old-fashioned striker, he entered League football with Wigan Athletic, scoring on his debut in a 3-1 win over Halifax Town in April 1980. Although he helped the Latics to promotion to the Third Division, he was released and joined Stockport County.

He made his debut in a 1-1 home draw against Peterborough United on the opening day of the 1982-83 season, of which at the end, he was the club's top scorer with 24 league goals including hat-tricks against Crewe Alexandra (Home 3-2) and Halifax Town (Home 4-2). He headed the club's scoring charts again in 1983-84 and scored another hat-trick against Crewe, this time in a 3-0 win at Gresty Road.

A great favourite with the Edgeley Park crowd, he had scored 41 goals in 70 League and Cup games when he was allowed to join Oldham Athletic. As with his former clubs, Quinn was the leading goalscorer but in March 1986, the struggling Lancashire club sold him to Portsmouth for £150,000. He helped the Fratton Park club to promotion but they were relegated after just one season. At the end of his contract, he opted to join Newcastle United, the fee of £680,000 being decided by the Transfer Tribunal. He made a sensational start for the Magpies, scoring four times on his debut against Leeds United and ended the campaign with 32 league goals.

In December 1992, after a spell on loan with Coventry City, he joined the Highfield Road club on a permanent basis and on the opening day of the 1993-94 season, scored a hat-trick at Highbury after ending the previous season as the club's leading scorer.

R

RAPID SCORING

On 6th January 1934, County met Halifax Town in a Third Division (North) fixture at Edgeley Park. The Hatters were enjoying a good season, lying second in the table, whilst the Shaymen were only three places behind them.

County played the first half with a strong wind at their backs but as half-time arrived, many of the 7,305 crowd felt their 2-0 advantage would not be enough. After the break, the Hatters scored an incredible eight goals in a 16 minute spell past a bemused Halifax 'keeper, Milton. The goal-scorers were:

Hill	(8 minutes)
Hill	(14 minutes)
Lythgoe	(50 minutes)
Hill	(51 minutes)
Vincent	(pen 53 minutes)
Foulkes	(57 minutes)
Downes	(59 minutes)
Stevenson	(61 minutes)
Downes	(65 minutes)
Downes	(66 minutes)
Lythgoe	(80 minutes)
Stevenson	(86 minutes)
Downes	(88 minutes)

RECEIPTS

The club's record receipts are £181,449 for the Coca Cola Cup semifinal first leg match against Middlesbrough at Edgeley Park on 26th February 1997.

RE-ELECTION

Stockport County lost their League status in 1904, finishing 16th out of 18 clubs, five points ahead of bottom club Leicester City who were re-elected. In the three previous seasons, Stockport had been 17th. In 1904-05 they won the Lancashire Combination and were successfully voted back into the Football League.

Since the formation of the Fourth Division in 1958, County have had to seek re-election on five occasions, in 1964-65, 1971-72, 1973-74, 1975-76 and 1984-85.

REFEREES

On 25th October 1924, County travelled to Fulham for a Second Division match and were losing 2-0 with six minutes still to play when the referee, Mr Bryan of Willenhall blew for full-time. Once off the pitch, a linesman told him of his error and he ordered both teams to return to the field of play in order to complete the remaining six minutes. When play did restart, County only had nine players as two had got changed and gone for a bath! The score remained at 2-0 in Fulham's favour but by then most of the crowd had gone home.

Another incident involving County and a referee was a tragic one and happened on 16th September 1972. The Edgeley Park club were losing 2-0 at Exeter City when the referee, Jim Finn of Chigwell Row, Essex, collapsed in the centre-circle after an hours play. On arrival at Exeter Hospital, the official was already dead. For the record County went on to lose 3-0 in a performance that was described by manager Brian Doyle as 'The worst since I took charge'.

REID, DUGGIE

A player of great power and skill, Duggie Reid made his first team debut for County on his 19th birthday and though he didn't score in a 4-1 win over Oldham Athletic, he won two penalties, of which only one was converted. Though he began his career as a half-back, he was switched to centre-forward but did not play in the championship decider against Lincoln City on the final day of the season as Joe Hill returned to the side.

During the war years, Reid made 38 appearances and began to attract the attention of the top clubs. In March 1946, Reid who had scored 26 goals, many from free-kicks in 91 League and Cup games, joined Portsmouth for £7,000.

He gave great service to the Fratton Park club over the next ten seasons and after scoring two goals on his debut in a 3-1 win over Blackburn Rovers on the opening day of the 1946-47 season, ended the campaign as the club's top scorer with 29 goals.

Reid went on to score eight hat-tricks for Pompey in a career that saw him score 135 goals in 327 first team games and win two League Championship medals.

RELEGATION

County have been relegated on five occasions. Their first taste came in 1920-21 when despite a Football League decision to relegate only one club, as the Third Division (South) would provide a promoted replacement, County finished bottom of the Second Division. County were in fact, undefeated in the final five games of the season, but four were drawn and by the time they played their last 'home' game at Old Trafford because Edgeley Park was suspended, the club were already doomed to last place. County were immediately promoted as champions of the Third Division (North) in 1921-22 and spent four seasons in the Second Division before being relegated a second time in 1925-26.

The club then spent 11 seasons in the Third Division (North) before winning promotion in 1936-37. Sadly they only spent one season in Division Two before being relegated for a third time. During this campaign they suffered one of their heaviest defeats when they lost 7-1 at Aston Villa. After 14 seasons in the Third Division, County were relegated a fourth time in 1958-59, this time to the Fourth Division. The club spent eight seasons in the League's basement before winning promotion in 1966-67. However, three seasons later the club were relegated for a fifth and thankfully last time when they finished bottom of the Third Division.

Since then, the club have had mixed fortunes, having to apply for re-election four times, winning promotion twice and appearing in four Play-offs at the end of a season!

RODGERS, NORMAN

Local amateur Norman Rodgers played his early football with Park Albion and Hooley Hill before joining Stockport County in November 1911. He made his debut at home to Bradford Park venue and scored County's goal in a 1-0 win. He was an instant success and in that 1911-12 season, scored 10 goals in 21 league games. At the end of the campaign he signed professional forms and in the three seasons prior to the outbreak of the First World War was the club's top scorer and the first County player to score 50 League goals. His best season was 1914-15 when he netted 21 goals in 35 league games including a spell of ten games in which he found the net eleven times.

During the war, the goal-scoring inside-forward scored 70 goals in 115 appearances. When League football resumed he continued to score on a regular basis but just nine days after his benefit match against Leicester City, Rodgers joined First Division Blackburn Rovers for a fee of £2,500. He had scored 76 goals in 164 League and Cup appearances.

Rovers hadn't won in ten games and looked like being relegated to the Second Division but Rodgers scored 13 goals in 11 games to help the club retain their top flight status. Injuries hampered his stay at Ewood Park and in the summer of 1923 he accepted that his career was over.

RUTTER, JOHN

After leaving school, Warrington-born John Rutter accepted an apprenticeship with Wolverhampton Wanderers and though in a three-year stay with the Molineux club he failed to win a place in the first team, he was on the bench during the club's Fairs Cup campaign in 1972-73. At the end of that season he joined Bournemouth on a free transfer but after only four games in the Cherries' first team he was on his way to Exeter City for a fee of £25,000. After an impressive first season, his progress was hampered by a cartilage operation and in the summer of 1976 after being released by the Devon club he was given a month's trial by County.

He was so impressive that he was an ever-present in his first two seasons with the Edgeley Park club and an automatic choice for the next ten years. A player who gave his all, John Rutter was never sent-off in a league match, his only blemish on a superb disciplinary record coming in a FA Cup match against Telford United when he was given his marching orders.

He appeared in 451 League and Cup games for the club, only one of three players to make over 400 appearances. With his playing career over, he worked for a property company before returning to Edgeley Park where he is now the club's Commercial Manager.

RYDEN, HUGH

Dumbarton-born Hugh Ryden was spotted scoring some spectacular goals by a Leeds United scout and after a successful trial, he signed for the Elland Road club. His first season with the Yorkshire club was spent in the youth side and he was in the reserves when Don Revie became manager. With his first team opportunities at Leeds limited, he moved to Bristol Rovers for a fee of £1,000.

After an injury-hit season in which he scored four goals in eight appearances, he was given a free transfer and in July 1963, he joined

Stockport County. After a good start in which he scored seven goals in nine games, his form slipped and he was allowed to move to Chester City.

It was at Sealand Road that Ryden enjoyed his most successful spell, scoring over 20 goals in his first season with the club. He spent three and a half seasons with Chester scoring 44 goals in 141 league games before Halifax Town paid £5,000 to take him to The Shay.

Plagued by injuries, he returned to Edgeley Park towards the end of the 1969-70 season for a second spell with the Hatters. It was Hugh Ryden who headed the only goal of the game as County beat First Division Crystal Palace 1-0 at Selhurst Park in a second round League Cup tie. However he suffered further injuries and after scoring 25 goals in 175 League and Cup appearances in his two spells, he retired from League football in 1973.

He later returned to Edgeley Park as Youth Team manager, a post he held for 18 months.

S

SALMON, MIKE

The Leyland-born goalkeeper began his career with Blackburn Rovers where he made just one Football League appearance. In 1982-83, still eligible for the FA Youth Cup, he went on loan to Chester and played in 18 League and Cup games before being given a free transfer by the Ewood Park club at the end of the season.

Following the retirement of County 'keeper Brian Lloyd, manager Eric Webster signed the 19-year-old Salmon and after making his debut in a 2-0 home defeat by York City on the opening day of the 1983-84 season, went on to make 134 consecutive appearances until he lost his place to Gary Walker.

He then joined Bolton Wanderers who were then a Third Division club but seven months and 36 games later he was back in the Fourth Division with Wrexham.

After 117 appearances in two and a half years at the Racecourse Ground, he moved to First Division Charlton Athletic for £100,000.

Now in his ninth season with the Addicks, the tried and tested 'keeper has played in almost 200 games.

SCOTCHBROOK, FRED

Horwich-born Fred Scotchbrook joined Bolton Wanderers just before the outbreak of the First World War but after only five appearances in the Wanderers' side, he decided he was not good enough for this standard of football and retired to concentrate on coaching. He remained at Burnden Park as coach and then assistant-secretary before joining Stockport County as manager in November 1924.

In 1924-25 County finished in a disappointing 19th place, only three points above the relegation position. Scotchbrook's second season with the club was even worse as they lost six of their firsts even fixtures and though he was sacked in February 1926, County still finished bottom of the Second Division, failing to win any of their away games.

His record at Edgeley Park did not deter Wolverhampton Wanderers from appointing him manager though he was never given full control at Molineux and became disheartened when directors would make decisions at a whim, which he could do nothing to prevent. Scotchbrook blamed the club's directors for the lack of success and left soon after criticising club policy at the annual meeting in the summer of 1927.

SECOND DIVISION

Stockport County have had five spells in the Second Division, although their last one followed the reorganisation of the Football League in 1992-93.

As Lancashire League champions, County were admitted to the Football League in 1900-01 and drew their first match at Leicester Fosse 2-2. In each of their first three seasons in the Second Division, the club finished 17th and so dropped into the Lancashire Combination for a year. A season later in 1905-06, they returned to the Second Division, where they remained until 1920-21 when they were relegated to the newly formed Third Division (North).

Promoted immediately, County began their third spell in the Sec-

ond Division in 1922-23 before suffering relegation again four seasons later. Promoted in 1936-37, the club's fourth spell in the Second
Division lasted just one season as they finished bottom of the League
with 31 points.

Following reorganisation in 1992-93, County's last spell in the 'Second' Division lasted five seasons and following the club's involve-
ment in the play-offs in 1992-93 and 1993-94, they eventually won
promotion to the First Division in 1996-97.

SHERLOCK, STEVE

Birmingham-born Steve Sherlock joined Manchester City in the summer of 1977 and though he was an ever-present in 1977-78 when the
Maine Road club's reserve side won the Central League championship, he was unable to displace Scottish international full-back Willie Donachie in the City first team. After being released by the Blues,
he joined Luton Town and made his debut for the other Hatters in a
6-1 win over Oldham Athletic on the opening day of the 1978-79 season. However, he only made one more first team appearance for the
Kenilworth Road club before joining County on a free transfer in
August 1979.

Forming an excellent full-back partnership with John Rutter, Sherlock went on to play in 273 League and Cup games for County over the
next seven seasons, scoring eight goals. An ever-present in 1981-82
he left Edgeley Park in the summer of 1986 when he joined Cardiff
City.

However, the popular left-back only made 15 appearances for the
Bluebirds before finding himself on loan at Newport County which
led to a permanent move in March 1987.

Sherwood's final season in football was 1987-88 which was also
Newport's last, as they were relegated to the Conference.

SHERPA VAN TROPHY

The competition for Associate Members of the Football League was
first sponsored for the 1987-88 season by Sherpa Van.

County's first match in the Sherpa Van Trophy saw them lose 5-2
on the artificial surface at Deepdale, the home of Preston North End
and after losing 3-1 at home to Bolton Wanderers, the club yet again
failed to qualify for the knockout stages. It was a similar story in

1988-89 for after drawing 1-1 at home to Crewe Alexandra, the Hatters went down 2-1 at Tranmere and so end their interest in the competition.

SMALLEST PLAYER

Although such statistics are always unreliable, especially for those players before the turn of the century, the distinction of being County's smallest player goes to Johnny Price. Standing at just 5ft 3ins and nicknamed 'Toppo' after the world famous puppet, the flying winger scored 27 goals in 345 League and Cup appearances for the club.

SMITH, JOE

Joe Smith was born in Dudley in 1889 and was a Newcastle St Luke's player when he was awoken one morning in August 1908, by Bolton trainer George Eccles. After making his debut at West Bromwich Albion in April 1909, he formed a left-wing partnership with Ted Vizard that played a major part in Bolton's success in that era.

He played in 51 wartime games for Bolton, scoring 48 goals including six against Stoke. He 'guested' for Chelsea along with Vizard and they helped the Stamford Bridge club win the London v Lancashire Cup Final. Smith, who won his first international cap in February 1913, continued his international career after the war but due to the hostilities, was limited to five appearances overall. In 1920-21 he scored 38 league goals, still a club record to equal Bert Freeman's League record at the time. In 1923 came Smith's greatest honour when he was the first FA Cup Final skipper to receive the trophy at Wembley. Three years later, he lifted the Cup again but his career at Bolton was coming to an end. After scoring 277 goals in 492 League and Cup games he joined Stockport County in March 1927, for £1,000.

He made his debut in a 2-2 home draw against Stoke City with only County chairman Ernest Barlow being aware that Smith's registration had not been received by the Football League. The club were fined £100 and for the only time in their history, had two points deducted for playing an 'unregistered player'.

The following season he scored 40 goals in 42 League and Cup appearances including becoming the first County player to score five goals in a match when Southport were beaten 6-3 on 7th January

1928. He repeated the feat in 1928-29 as Lincoln City were defeated 7-3. By the time he left Edgeley Park in May 1929, Joe Smith had scored 63 goals in 73 games and netted a remarkable eight hat-tricks.

Smith then joined Darwen and had a spell at Manchester Central before becoming manager of Reading in July 1931. In August 1935, he became Blackpool's manager, a position he held until April 1958, when he was the longest-serving manager in the League. Smith guided the Seasiders to their best-ever League position and to a FA Cup Final win in 1953 against Bolton!

SPONSORS

The club's present sponsors are Robinson's Beers whilst previous sponsors have included Cobra Lagers, Gordon Ford Group and Langdale Services.

STANIFORTH, RON

A tall and cultured full-back, Ron Staniforth was equally at home at right or left back and after making his County debut in a 4-0 home win over Tranmere Rovers in November 1946, went on to give some brilliant displays. Over the next six seasons, Staniforth made 245 League and Cup appearances, his only goal giving County the points in a 1-0 win against Accrington Stanley in April 1950.

In the summer of 1952, Staniforth followed former County manager Andy Beattie to Huddersfield Town for a fee of £8,000. He helped the Leeds Road club to win promotion from the Second Division and reach a highest place of third in the First Division. In 1954 he won eight full caps for England in the space of nine months. In the summer of 1955 he joined Sheffield Wednesday and in his first season helped the club win the Second Division title. He had appeared in 118 League and Cup games for the Owls when he lost his place to Charlie Johnson and joined Barrow, first as player-manager and then as manager. He later had a spell at Hillsborough on the training staff before leaving the game for good.

STEVENSON, JIMMY

An important member of County's most successful attack, Jimmy Stevenson was a scheming inside-left who not only became a maker of chances but was also a consistent marksman in his own right.

The son of a steel worker he began work as an engineer after leaving school and finished his apprenticeship after signing for Scottish Second Division club Third Lanark. Three years later, he moved south of the border to play for Second Division South Shields and after scoring 24 goals in 54 league appearances he moved on to Bradford City. Things didn't work out for him at Valley Parade and after a short time he joined Aldershot who were then members of the Southern League.

He signed for Stockport in the summer of 1932 and made his debut on the opening day of the 1932-33 season, scoring one of County's goals in a 5-1 home win over Darlington. When Halifax Town were beaten 13-0 in January 1934, it was Stevenson who set up many of the chances converted by Downes, Hill, Lythgoe and Foulkes and not to be outdone, scored two of the goals himself. He had scored 43 goals in 110 League and Cup appearances when ligament trouble ended his playing career.

He then had a brief spell in charge of Macclesfield Town before returning to Edgeley Park to become the club's reserve-team trainer.

STEWART, FRED

Fred Stewart was involved in the administrative side of Stockport County for a number of years before becoming the club's first manager following their successful application to join the Football League in 1900. Despite Stewart's shrewd dealings in the transfer market, County struggled to stay in the League and finally lost their place in 1904 when they were not re-elected and went to play in the Lancashire Combination. A year later they returned to the League with Stewart not only guiding them to tenth place, their best-ever League position, but also helping the club make a profit of 500 on the season.

In May 1911, Fred Stewart was engaged by Cardiff City to become their first secretary-manager. He immediately brought a wealth of professional experience and knowledge to Ninian Park and in 1913, the club won the Second Division of the Southern League. Stewart seemed capable of bringing in better players as the Welsh club improved in status and following their League entry in 1920 he brought international players from all over the country to Ninian Park.

Amazingly, Fred Stewart still found time to build up a number of business interests, although he was seldom at any of his premises. City missed the League Championship by a whisker in 1923-24, were beaten finalists in the 1925 FA Cup Final and in 1927 reached their nadir with the FA Cup Final victory over Arsenal – it proved to be the pinnacle of Fred Stewart's career. He decided to retire from football in 1933 and concentrate on his businesses.

SUBSTITUTES

The first-ever Stockport County substitute was Frank Beaumont who came on for Dennis Hoggart against Chester at Sealand Road on 21st August 1965. The club had to wait until the 14th game of the 1969-70 season for the first goal-scoring substitute – Peter Bebbington scoring in the 3-1 home defeat by Mansfield Town.

The greatest number of substitutes used in a single season by Stockport under the single substitute rule was 36 but from 1986-87, two substitutes were allowed and in 1988-89, 58 were used. For the last few seasons, three substitutes have been allowed and in 1997-98, 88 were used.

The greatest number of substitute appearances for County has been made by Andy Mutch who has come on in 36 League games with six more in cup ties. It was in seasons 1996-97 and 1997-98 that Andy Mutch rewrote the Stockport record on the matter of substitutes with an extraordinary 18 league appearances in the substitute's shirt in each season!

SUMMERBEE, MIKE

A West Country boy from a footballing family, he played in more than 200 games for Swindon Town, helping them clinch promotion from Division Three in 1963. His dashing excursions along the wings caught the eye of some of the bigger clubs and in August 1965, this te-nacious winger became the first of Joe Mercer's signings at Manches-ter City. In his first season at Maine Road he helped City win the Second Division title and then in a three-year spell between 1968 and 1970 – the most successful period in the club's history – he played a significant role in City's triumphs. An England international, win-ning eight caps, he scored 67 goals in 441 games for City before join-ing Burnley. In his only full season at Turf Moor, the Clarets were relegated and in December 1976, he moved to Blackpool. After only three appearances at Bloomfield Road he joined Stockport County in the summer of 1977.

In March 1978, following the dismissal of Alan Thompson, he was appointed player-manager and though he signed Les Bradd and Stuart Lee who netted 38 goals between them, County could only finish in a disappointing 17th place. After a poor start to the 1979-80 campaign and a 6-1 defeat at Bradford City, Summerbee resigned as manager and did not play for the club again, having scored seven goals in 101 appearances.

SUNDAY FOOTBALL

The first-ever Sunday matches in the Football League took place on 20th January 1974, during the three-day week imposed by the Government, during the trail of strength with the coal-miners.

County entertained Doncaster Rovers on that date and though the crowd of 4,050 was the club's highest of the season, the game was goal-less. Though the Hatters ended that 1973-74 season bottom of the Fourth Division and had to apply for re-election, they won one and drew three of their four matches played on the 'Sabbath'.

SWORD, TOMMY

Bishop Auckland-born forward Tommy Sword topped the Northern League scoring charts with 35 goals for his home-town club before signing for managerless Stockport County in November 1979. After coming on as a substitute in a 1-0 home win over Walsall, he returned to his native north-east for his first full game, scoring both goals in a 2-1 win over Hartlepool United. Following an injury to Les Bradd, he switched to play centre-half, occasionally returning to play as an emergency centre-forward.

On 21st November 1981, Sword broke his leg in County's 3-1 FA Cup win over Mossley and was out of the side for over 12 months. Thankfully, he made a successful return to the County side and over the next three seasons, missed just nine games. Despite playing as a central defender it didn't stop him scoring goals and in 1984-85 he was the club's top scorer with 12 goals. Sword was also a consistent penalty-taker, scoring 18 times from the spot in three seasons.

In the summer of 1986 he left Edgeley Park to join Hartlepool United for £5,000 but within six months he was back playing for his beloved County. He made his final appearance for the club as a substitute in a 2-1 home win over Torquay United in November 1987. One of the most respected players in the club's post-war era, Tommy Sword scored 55 goals in 270 first team games before being granted a well-deserved testimonial against Manchester City.

T

TALLEST PLAYER

The tallest player ever on County's books has to be Kevin Francis. At 6ft 7ins, 'Big Kev' provided the fans with their first-ever 'cult' figure and, excluding wartime games, he became only the third County player to have scored over 100 goals.

THIRD DIVISION

Stockport County have had five spells in the Third Division. Relegated in 1920-21, County's first spell in the Third Division lasted just one season as they won the championship with 56 points. The Hatters made a tremendous start, winning their first four matches and were unbeaten in their first six. From New Year's Eve 1921 until the Easter weekend, the club enjoyed a run of 15 games without defeat and clinched the title with two games left, to become the first champions of the Northern Section.

The club's second spell began in 1926-27 but after losing their opening game of that campaign 4-1 at Halifax Town, it was evident that a return to the Second Division was not going to be easy. In fact, County's second spell lasted 11 seasons and though they finished runners-up in 1928-29 and 1929-30 and third on another three occasions, only the champions went up and County had to wait until 1936-37. Sadly, they finished bottom of the Second Division in their first season and so began their third spell in 1938-39. This time county spent 14 seasons in the Third Division before being relegated to the League's basement in 1958-59.

County were promoted to the Third Division in 1966-67 but their fourth spell lasted just three seasons before they were relegated in 1969-70. It was 1990-91 before the club regained their Third Division status and after finishing fifth the following season, were involved in the end of season play-offs. Following the reorganisation of the Football League for 1992-93, County found themselves playing in the Second Division, winning promotion as runners-up to Bury in 1996-97.

THOMPSON, ALAN

Liverpool-born Alan Thompson began his league career with Sheffield Wednesday during a period of decline for the Hillsborough club. He made 173 appearances for the Owls, who had sunk into the Third Division by the time he joined Stockport County in the summer of 1976.

He made his debut in the opening game of the 1976-77 season, scoring the only goal of the game in a 1-0 win at Newport County. That season he made 43 league appearances and scored six goals but in April 1977, when Eddie Quigley was sacked, he was surprisingly appointed player-manager at the age of 25.

County's youngest manager brought in the experienced Mike Summerbee and by the end of February 1978, County were fourth in Division Four. There followed three successive defeats, after which Thompson lost his managerial position! He continued to play for County for another year but after scoring 18 goals in 108 games he left Edgeley Park to play in America. He later returned to these shores to play for Bradford City before ending his career with Scunthorpe United.

THORPE, ANDY

Playing in almost every position in his 14 years service with the club, Andy Thorpe broke Bob Murray's record number of appearances and when he was released in the summer of 1992 he had played in 555 games.

Eddie Quigley signed Thorpe as an apprentice and after serving his time in the reserves, he made his first team debut in a friendly against Fort Lauderdale Strikers in February 1978. A couple of months later he made his league debut at right-back in a 2-0 defeat at Hartlepool

United. During his first spell with the club, for he had 17 months with Tranmere Rovers where he was signed by Frank Worthington and sold back by John king, he made 314 league appearances under six managers. Between 29 September 1980, and 21 April 1984, he made an unbroken run of 169 league matches.

Thorpe's first four games for his new club saw him play against County on three occasions but in January 1988, after playing in 62 games for the Prenton Park club he rejoined the Hatters.

After helping the club win promotion from the Fourth Division in

Andy Thorpe

1990-91, his last season in League football was spent in the Third Division where on 12th October 1991, he broke Bob Murray's 28 year old appearance record in the match at Birmingham City.

At the end of the season he moved to Australia but after just 10 games 'Down Under' he suffered a serious Achilles tendon injury, the worst of his career. He returned to England and teamed up with Oshor Williams at Witton Albion.

Voted Club-man of the Year in his last season at Edgeley Park, Andy Thorpe is one of the club's most popular personalities.

TODD, LEE

Diminutive left-back Lee Todd joined Stockport County on a free transfer from Hartlepool United juniors in the summer of 1990 and made his first team debut in a 3-0 home win over Walsall on 1st September 1990. In his first two seasons at Edgeley Park, Todd played in a variety of positions before establishing himself in the County defence in 1992-93.

Todd appeared in all of the club's Wembley appearances in the Autoglass Trophy and play-off finals and in 1996-97 was an important member of the County side that won promotion to the First Division and reached

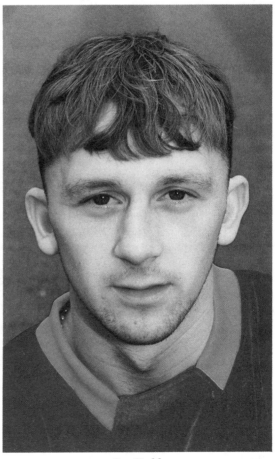

Lee Todd

the semi-finals of the League Cup where they lost 2-1 on aggregate to Middlesbrough.

A real crowd pleaser, the all-action style of this raiding left-back was sorely missed at Edgeley Park when he followed his manager Dave Jones to Southampton in the 1997 close season after appearing in 300 games for the Hatters.

TRANSFERS

One of the most unusual arrangements involving the transfer of a Stockport County player occurred in 1927. Manchester United persuaded the Hatters to allow amateur wing-half Hughie McLenahan to join them in exchange for three freezers of ice cream. United scout Louis Rocca arranged for these to be given to the County club to raise club funds at their bazaar!

On 19th October 1951, Jack Connor, County's leading marksman and his wife were in a Bradford cinema when a message was flashed across the screen 'Would Jack Connor, Bradford City's centre-forward please go to the foyer'. There he was met by County manager Andy Beattie and club chairman Ernest Barlow who persuaded him to sign there and then for a fee of £2,500.

The club's current record signing is Paul Cook who cost £250,000 when signed from Tranmere Rovers in October 1997. The record transfer fee received is £1.6m from Middlesbrough for Alun Armstrong in February 1998.

TRAUTMANN, BERT

Arriving in England in April 1945, it was at a Prisoner of War camp at Ashton-in-Makerfield that Bert Trautmann first tried his hand at goal-keeping. He began his career with St Helens Town and after some impressive displays signed for Manchester City. Replacing the great Frank Swift, he was a member of the victorious City side of 1956 that won the FA Cup beating Birmingham City 3-1 at Wembley. Trautmann played for the last 15 minutes with a broken neck! Also in 1956 he was voted the Footballer of the Year. He went on to make 545 appearances for the Maine Road club before playing for non-League Wellington Town.

At Edgeley Park, Trautmann held a number of management positions which were classed as 'administrative' and 'general' but there is no doubt that he had some authority. His period with County coincided with the arrival of Chairman Vic Bernard but despite the success of turning 'Friday Night' into 'County Night', Trautmann had left the club before they were promoted in 1967.

U

UNDEFEATED

Stockport County have remained undefeated at home throughout three League seasons: 1927-28, 1928-29 and 1933-34. The club's best and longest undefeated sequence at Edgeley Park in the Football League is of 48 matches between 16th April 1927, and 5th October 1929. County's longest run of undefeated Football League matches home and away is 18 between 28th January 1933, and 2nd September 1933.

UTILITY PLAYERS

A utility player is one of those particularly gifted footballers who can play in several, or even many, different positions. Eddie Vincent, who made his County debut in March 1929, developed from a utility player into a fine defender capable of occupying all five defensive positions, which he did. Arthur Burrows who played for County either side of the Second World War played in every outfield position except full-back. Bob Murray who played in 495 League and Cup games for the club was an outstanding half-back but he was more than capable of playing at full-back or inside-forward. Fred Goodwin played in almost every position for the club, even replacing the injured Alan Ogley in goal in a match at Orient whilst Billy Haydock also showed his versatility by playing at half-back, inside-forward or full-back.

After the mid 1960s, players were encouraged to become more adaptable and to see their roles as less stereotyped. At the same time, however, much less attention came to be paid to the implication of wearing a certain numbered shirt and accordingly some of the more versatile players came to wear almost all the different numbered shirts at some stage or another, although this did not necessarily indicate a vast variety of positions. In the modern game, the club's record appearance holder, Andy Thorpe wore every outfield shirt except Number nine.

V

VICTORIES IN A SEASON – HIGHEST

In the 1928-29 and 1929-30 seasons, Stockport County won 28 of their 42 fixtures to finish runners-up in the Third Division (North) on each occasion.

VICTORIES IN A SEASON – LOWEST

Stockport County's poorest performance was in 1969-70 when they won only six matches out of their 46 games and finished bottom of the Third Division.

W

WARD, PETER

Peter Ward began his career in his native north-east with Chester-le-Street before signing for Huddersfield Town in January 1987. He never really established himself at Leeds Road, making 42 appearances for the Yorkshire club in two years before moving to Rochdale on a free transfer.

In his first season at Scotland, he helped Rochdale to the fifth round of the FA Cup and went on to appear in 96 League and Cup games before joining Stockport County in June 1991.

An excellent passer of the ball, Ward liked nothing better than to be involved in the hurly-burly of central midfield. He made his County debut in a 5-0 home win over Swansea City on the opening day of the

Peter Ward

1991-92 season. A virtual ever-present over the next four seasons, he was made captain in 1992-93 and led the club to the play-offs and a Wembley appearance in the final of the Autoglass Trophy. Though never scoring enough goals, when he did get his name on the score sheet, they were usually goals to remember. In that seasons play-off semi-final first leg, his swerving free-kick gave County a 1-0 win against Stoke City.

He went on to appear in 183 games for County when in July 1995, he joined Wrexham for a fee of £50,000.

WARTIME FOOTBALL

In spite of the outbreak of war in 1914, the major football leagues embarked upon their planned programme of matches for the ensuing season and these were completed on schedule at the end of April the following year. The season saw County finish 14th in the Second Division with Norman Rodgers becoming the club's first player to score 20 league goals in a season.

In the summer of 1915, the Football League was suspended and County participated in the Lancashire Section. They fared quite well in the season of wartime football finishing fifth in the Principal Tournament. In 1916-17 the Lancashire Section was expanded to 16 teams and County who only lost five of their 30 games, finished runners-up to Liverpool. The penultimate wartime season, 1917-18, saw the introduction of playing each team home and away on successive weeks and a good season ended with County in sixth place. In the last wartime season, County finished in eighth place, their lowest position in four seasons of regionalised football. With the end of the hostilities and the gradual return of the surviving armed forces, the regionalised football season petered out.

In contrast to the events of 1914, once war was declared on 3rd September 1939, the Football League programme of 1939-40 was immediately suspended and the government forbade any major sporting events, so that for a while there was no football of any description.

A wartime regional League was eventually established and County were allocated to the Western Section. Four games early in the 1939-40 season gave the club an indication of the ups and downs of wartime football. In consecutive matches, County beat Tranmere Rovers

5-0 with Duggie Reid scoring four goals, drew 6-6 at Manchester City with Grimsby Town's 'guest' Fred Howe netting four of the goals and lost 7-4 at home to Manchester United with Duggie Reid hitting another hat-trick. County then travelled to Chester and were beaten 8-1.

Most of the club's games during the Second World War were poorly attended although the inclusion of a number of famous 'guests' gave the spectators an interest.

In 1940-41 Manchester City, who scored 104 goals, more than any other team beat County 9-1 at Edgeley Park with Alex Herd, later to play in 119 League and Cup games for the Hatters, scoring four of the goals! Later that season, County lost 12-3 on aggregate to Blackpool in the Football League War Cup with the Seasiders centre-forward Jack Dodds scoring eight goals in their 9-2 win at Bloomfield Road.

Although the Second World War ended in 1945, the Football League didn't resume until the following year and so in 1945-46, County made history as participants in the Third Division (North) Cup meeting against Doncaster Rovers at Edgeley Park. The first leg at Belle Vue had ended all-square at 2-2 but after the match ended in a draw after extra-time, the two teams were asked to settle the outcome that day. The first team to score would win, but the scores were still level after 203 minutes when the game was abandoned through bad light!

WATERALL, ALBERT

One of three footballing brothers, Albert Waterall had considerable First Division experience with Notts County before joining Stockport in 1913. He arrived at Edgeley Park as an inside-forward but soon showed his versatility by playing at half-back. Though he only completed one season 1920-21 as the club's top scorer, he played for County for 13 successive seasons including the war years. After the hostilities were over, Waterall continued to turn out for County, going on to play in 300 League and Cup games for the club and scoring 36 goals.

He left Edgeley Park in the close season of 1926 after County had been relegated to the Third Division. He joined Leyton Orient but only made two appearances before deciding to hang up his boots.

WEBB, BILLY

Within a month of joining his first League club, Rochdale, left-back Billy Webb was on his way to Second Division Leicester City for a fee of £1,250. During six years at Filbert Street, Webb's career was interrupted by injuries and National Service and in the summer of 1957 he joined Stockport County on a free transfer.

He made his debut in a 2-1 defeat at Bradford City on the opening day of the season and was one of only two ever-presents as County finished ninth in the Third Division (North). Webb was also ever-present in 1959-60 and went on to appear in 262 League and Cup games before leaving Edgeley Park in July 1963, to play non-League football for Hyde United.

WEBSTER, ERIC

After serving two years National Service, he signed full-time professional for Manchester City in February 1952, but his only first team appearance for the club was in a 6-0 defeat at Cardiff City. He then did the rounds in non-League football, playing for Ashton United, Hyde United and Macclesfield before moving to Wales to play for Nantlle Vale and Pwllheli.

He then joined Stalybridge Celtic and after Freddie Pye was sacked, Webster was promoted to his first managerial position. Sadly, he too was sacked shortly afterwards and he moved to take charge at Hyde United. After three seasons he was dismissed, as he was at Runcorn some twelve months later. Webster then returned to another former club, Ashton United where he resigned after just one season.

Webster arrived at Edgeley Park in 1974 as grounds-man before being invited to look after the club's youngsters. Four years later, he was appointed Mike Summerbee's assistant-manager and later supported Jimmy McGuigan in this capacity before being made manager in May 1982.

During his three years in charge, County struggled near the foot of Division Four, their highest position being 16th in 1983-84. After being replaced by Colin Murphy in August 1985, he continued to serve a succession of County managers and find talented players who because of the club's financial problems could later be sold to bring in much needed money.

In 16 years at Edgeley Park, Eric Webster proved himself to be one of the club's greatest servants.

WESTGARTH, FRED

Fred Westgarth never played League football and first arrived at Edgeley Park from South Shields as a trainer in 1926. He then worked as a coach with Ebbw Vale, Workington and Luton Town before breaking into club management with Stockport County.

Inheriting most of the players who had gone close to winning the Third Division (North) championship in 1933-34, Westgarth could only lead County to a disappointing seventh place in 1934-35. However, he did produce the club's best Cup-fighting team when despite having to play seven games, they reached the fifth round of the FA Cup for the first time. Also that season, County beat Walsall 2-0 at Maine Road to win the Northern Section Cup.

In 1935-36 County finished in fifth place but in September 1936, Westgarth resigned to be replaced by Carlisle's Bob Kelly. Three months later, the Cumbrian club replaced Kelly with Westgarth. He only stayed a short while at Brunton Park before on to take charge at Bradford City. He took them to third place in the Third Division (North) but in 1943 he surprisingly left Valley Parade to manage Hartlepool United.

Here he found great success, moulding together a team which gave the club its finest years. After finishing fifth in 1954-55 and fourth in 1955-56, they probably would have won the Third Division (North) title but for his death the following season, in which they finished runners-up.

WHITE, LEN

A former Yorkshire miner, Len White was handed Jackie Milburn's shirt by Newcastle's directors in something of a gamble. Previously very much an outside-right who never really showed his potential, he grabbed the opportunity and went on the rampage in the next five seasons. In fact, only Milburn has scored more goals for the Magpies than Len White.

Tyneside soon warmed to his rip-roaring style and by the end of the

1957-58 season he was being strongly tipped to play for England but the international call never came. He did score an eight-minute hat-Trick for the Football League and went on to score 153 goals in 269 League and Cup games before joining Huddersfield Town in February 1962.

After scoring 39 goals in 110 games for the Yorkshire club, White signed for Stockport County and in a fourth round FA Cup tie at Liverpool, he headed the Hatters in front even though the Anfield side later equalised and won the replay. In 1965-66 he topped the club's scoring charts with 15 goals in 33 League games including a memorable hat-trick in County's record 7-1 away victory at Bradford City. After scoring 25 goals in 58 first team appearances, County released White, which was a shame, for the following season, the club won the Fourth Division championship, which would have been a fitting end to Len White's career.

WILLIAMS, ALBERT

Although he wasn't a regular member of the Stockport County first team, making just six appearances in the 1903-04 season, he was forced to retire from playing as a result of an injury. After a spell as the club's trainer, he was promoted to manager in 1919 when David Ashworth left the club.

His first 18 months in charge coincided with a disastrous spell for the club which culminated in them being relegated in 1920-21 with only 30 points as they finished bottom of Division Two.

Williams signed proven goal-scorer Ernie Simms, winger Ben Boardman and another goal-scorer in Bob Blood. County then won the Third Division (North) championship at their first attempt, conceding only 21 goals all season. The following season though, they missed relegation by one place. After a respectable place of 13th in 1923-24, a dreadful run of results in the autumn of 1924 saw Williams resign his post.

WILLIAMS, BILL

Bill Williams started his League career with Rochdale, signing professional forms in August 1981. Initially playing in midfield he was switched to the centre of defence in his second season and soon became a cultured defender. He played in 95 league games for the Scotland club before following team-mate Les Chapman to Edgeley Park in the summer of 1985.

He made his debut in a 2-2 home draw against Chester in September 1985, but after playing in 120 League and Cup games, he was transferred to First Division neighbours Manchester City for £50,000. Within a couple of months and after making only one substitute appearance at Ipswich Town in the unfamiliar position of right-back, he was back at Edgeley Park for a cut-price fee of £30,000.

Returning to his proper central defensive role, he continued to give outstanding performances and was a regular member of County's successful teams of the early 1990s, playing in all of the club's four visits to Wembley. The last of these against Burnley in the 1994 play-offs, was his final outing in County colours.

Williams, who played in 314 League and Cup games for the Hatters in his two spells with the club, was offered a contract to stay at Edgeley Park, but he opted to leave and work in the family's decorating business.

WILLIAMS, OSHOR

After beginning his career with one of his local clubs, Middlesbrough, he left Ayresome Park to sign professional forms for Manchester United in August 1976. But with so many international stars around, his progress was slow, although he did make the first team squad and so lowering his sights, he returned to the north-east and linked up with non-League Gateshead.

It was his performances for them that came to the notice of Southampton's Geordie manager Lawrie McMenemy and the big man paid £2,000 to take him to The Dell. However, there was be to be more frustration as Southampton loaned him out to Exeter City at the start of the 1978-79 season and it was with the Grecians that he finally got his chance in League soccer. He made his debut as a substitute against Brentford in September 1978, but after three appearances it was back to reserve football with the Saints until March 1979, when he made his First Division against Arsenal. There followed another loan spell with Reading but when Stockport went in with a £10,000 bid for his transfer, he agreed to what was his sixth transfer in three years!

The first black player to join County, he made his debut at Tranmere Rovers in August 1979. Over the next five seasons he notched up 216 League and Cup appearances for the Edgeley Park club, scoring 31 goals.

A favourite with the fans, he was disappointed when the club failed to improve the salary he had received when he first joined the club and played on a month-to-month contract until Port Vale signed him. At the end of his second season with the

Oshor Williams

club, he helped the Valiants win promotion but in the summer of 1986 he returned to the north-west to play for Preston North End. Injury finished his career at the age of 29 but he stayed on at Deepdale as the club's Community Development Officer before coaching spells with Halifax Town, Winsford United and Witton Albion.

WILMOTT, GORDON

Gordon Wilmott started his football career with Bagthorpe Athletic in the North Notts. League and at the age of 14, signed for Nottingham Forest as an amateur. On his 18th birthday he signed professional forms for Birmingham City but in the summer of 1948 and after having failed to break into the St Andrew's club's first team, he joined Stockport County.

Despite only averaging 19 games a season during his first five years at Edgeley Park, he eventually established himself as the club's regular centre-half during the 1953-54 season. By the end of that campaign he had been made captain. Wilmott went on to play in 219 League and Cup games for County, playing his last game in March 1959. It was in his last season that he scored his only goal for the club when he gave County the lead at Tranmere only for them to eventually lose the game 3-1.

After joining Crewe Alexandra for £1,000, Wilmott's career was cut short by a displaced disc in his spine and on retiring in 1961, he remained at Gresty Road as the club's chief scout.

WILSON, ANDREW

Arriving at Sheffield Wednesday from Clyde in 1900, Andrew Wilson took a little time to settle but even so he ended his first season at the club as the leading scorer with 13 goals. In a career that spanned 20 years, Wilson was leading scoring in eight of his 16 seasons with the Owls, scoring 216 goals in 545 League and Cup games. He won League Championship medals in 1902-03 and 1903-04 and scored twice in the FA Cup semi-final of 1907 as Woolwich Arsenal were beaten 3-1 and then set up Simpson's winning goal in the final itself. Wilson won six full caps for Scotland, the first coming against England in 1907. During the First World War he appeared in a further 75 games for Wednesday, scoring 25 goals and when league football resumed in 1919-20 he played in just one more game before retiring to concentrate on a career in management.

A quiet, deep-thinking man, his first managerial post was at Bristol Rovers but in five seasons at Eastville he did little and resigned when Rovers just missed re-election in 1925-26. He then took charge at Oldham Athletic and almost led them to promotion in 1929-30 but the Boundary Park club lost their last game at Barnsley to finish third.

In July 1932, Wilson became manager of Stockport County and in his first and only season with the club, took them to within five points of the Third Division (North) championship. County scored 99 goals that season, including eight in Wilson's last match in charge, an 8-5 victory over Chester!

WILSON, GENE

Standing just 5ft 4ins, diminutive winger Gene Wilson began his career with Worksop Town in the Midland League before doing his National Service in the Far East. On his release, he had spells with Sheffield Wednesday and Rotherham United before joining County as a part-time professional in the summer of 1954. During his stay at Millmoor he had been switched from inside-forward to winger with great success and it was in this position that he made his County debut in a goal-less draw at home to Grimsby Town in September 1954.

Though he scored his fair share of goals during his eight seasons with the club, 47 in 239 League and Cup games, he provided all County's forwards with excellent service.

In March 1962, Wilson was playing for County's 'A' team against Manchester City 'A' team after being told to get himself fit following an ankle injury. During the game, he was sent-off for arguing with the referee. Reluctant to leave the field, he was told by the referee, that if he hadn't left the pitch after 10 seconds, the game would be abandoned. He prolonged his departure sufficiently for the referee to carry out his threat and abandon the game.

Wilson was sacked and saw out the rest of his career playing non-League football for Stalybridge Celtic, Wigan, Altrincham and Llandudno.

WOODS, MATT

Matt Woods was a dominating centre-half who, in the 1950s, made up an excellent half-back line with Ronnie Clayton and Mick McGrath at Ewood Park. He had joined Blackburn Rovers after just eight appearances for his first club, Everton, finding first team opportunities limited.

In seven seasons with Rovers, Woods played in 307 first team games, scoring three goals before emigrating to Australia after losing his place to Mike England.

On his return to England, he played 34 league games for Luton

Town, one of which was a 4-1 defeat at Edgeley Park. After the game, Eddie Quigley and Bert Trautmann sold the club to Woods and at the end of that 1965-66 season, he joined County as captain.

Forming a formidable partnership with Eddie Stuart in the heart of the County defence, he was an ever-present as County won the Fourth Division championship. A serious knee injury ended his career at the age of 37, though he did try to make a comeback with Drumcondra, flying over to Ireland at the weekends for games.

Woods then had a spell in charge at Altrincham but after six months he was sacked and returned to Edgeley Park as coach to Walter Galbraith. Six months later, he found himself in charge and in 1970-71, his first season at the helm, the club finished 11th in the Fourth Division. He was sacked midway through his second season after a defeat by Blyth Spartans in the FA Cup.

WORLD WIDE WEB

Stockport supporters can now get up-to-date information direct to their PC, courtesy of the Internet. The address (URL) of the official Internet web site is:

http://www.stockportmbc.gov.uk/County/

There is also an unofficial "Hatters Online" at:

http://www.keppler.demon.co.uk/stockport/

WORST START

The club's worst ever start to a season was in 1964-65. It took 13 League games to record the first victory of the season, drawing two and losing 10 of the opening fixtures. The run ended with a 2-1 success over Aldershot at Edgeley Park on 10th October 1964. The club though continued to have a dismal season, ending the campaign bottom of the Fourth Division.

'X'

In football 'X' traditionally stands for a draw. The club record for the number of draws in a season was in 1988-89 when they managed 21 draws out of 46 matches.

XMAS DAY

There was a time when football matches were regularly played on Christmas Day but in recent years, the game's authorities have dropped the fixture from their calendar.

The club's first League game on Christmas Day was in 1902 when the Hatters travelled the short distance to play Glossop and lost 3-0. In fact, of the eight league games played on Christmas Day before the First World War, County only won one, 2-1 at home to Leeds City in 1907. Between the wars, County won half of their 16 Christmas Day fixtures and in 1930, Frank Newton scored the club's first Christmas Day hat-trick as Gateshead were beaten 3-1.

In the first Christmas Day fixture after the Second World War, Bill Brown scored a hat-trick in a 4-1 win at Rochdale. Ray Haddington netted a hat-trick in 1951 as the Hatters beat Crewe Alexandra 4-2 at Edgeley Park.

On Christmas Day 1956, Ray Drake scored the club's fastest-ever goal in the 2-1 home win over Accrington Stanley and a year later the club played its last league game on Christmas Day as Darlington were beaten 4-1.

YOUNGEST PLAYER

The youngest player to appear in a first-class fixture for Stockport County is Steve Massey who came on as a substitute for Norman

Lloyd in a Fourth Division match against Darlington (Home 2-1) on 28th February 1975, when he was 16 years 337 days old.

Z

ZENITH

Taking "zenith" in its literal meaning of "highest point", few fans will argue over which season has been the finest in the club's history. In 1996-97, Stockport County became a household name thanks to their great Coca Cola Cup exploits. After reaching the semi-finals of the competition, where they eventually bowed out to Middlesbrough, the Hatters took their excellent cup form into the League to seal the runners-up spot in the Second Division.

In 1997-98, the club finished eighth in the First Division, their highest-ever Football League placing.

We publish a wide range of local interest books covering all of the North West, and throughout most of Britain. Here is a small selection:

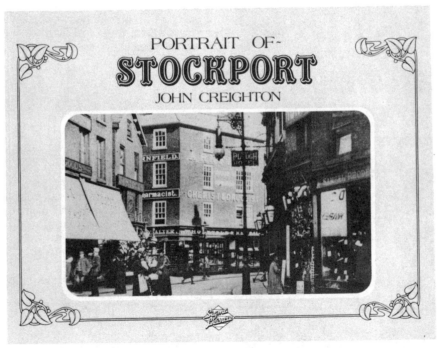

PORTRAIT OF STOCKPORT

Stockport has many claims to fame, and most of them are documented in this classic book. Read about the massive railway bridge, the many historic buildings and even the system of caves beneath the shopping streets. Fully illustrated.

£6.95

BLEAK & BLUE:
22 YEARS AT THE MANCHESTER ACADEMY OF FOOTBALL FARCE

30,000 people can't be wrong - or maybe they are! Craig Winstanley wrtes his heartfelt account of what could again be a great football club! **Share the joys and misery** of two decades spent in supporting Manchester City Football Club. **Boggle at the Blues record**: fifteen managers, two cup finals, two promotions and three relegations. **A big book in every way!** All major games covered in relentless detail. **Hugely entertaining:** you'll laugh, you'll cry - mostly the latter! *£8.95!*

COME ON CYMRU!
FOOTBALL IN WALES

"Keith Haynes is the Welsh Nick Hornby . . . you won't put this book down until you've read it from cover to cover." - *Future* magazine. **The first book** to be written by fans of Welsh football for football fans everywhere. **Includes contributions** from leading Welsh fanzine writers. **The highs and the lows** of Welsh football, nationally and internationally. **An entertaining read** - even for non-Welsh-football supporters! £6.95

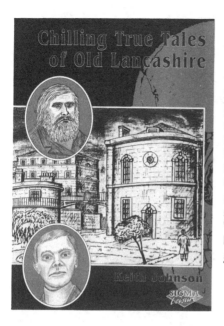

CHILLING TRUE TALES OF OLD LANCASHIRE

Draw the curtains, snuggle up by the fire and prepare yourself for a fright or two!

Northern author Keith Johnson has assembled a collection of stories to make your blood run cold. Just the thing after watching your favourite soccer team on a cold, winter afternoon!

Set in Victorian Lancashire, this is a spine-chilling collection of tales - "...sure to thrill, chill and amaze" THE LANCASTER GUARDIAN

£6.95.

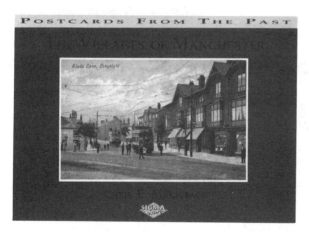

POSTCARDS FROM THE PAST: THE VILLAGES OF MANCHESTER

This nostalgic tour of the suburbs of Manchester is based on rare postcards of former villages and hamlets. Written by well-known local historian Chris Makepeace, the book includes street scenes, social history and notable buildings. Truly a collector's item!

£6.95

I REMAIN, YOUR SON JACK:
LETTERS FROM THE FIRST WORLD WAR

This collection of letters and photographs was found in a shoe box by local author Sheila Morten. They have been presented in book format to reflect the experiences of an ordinary Stockport soldier. **"Author and publisher deserve credit for a painstaking piece of historical research"** STOCKPORT HERITAGE. *£8.95*

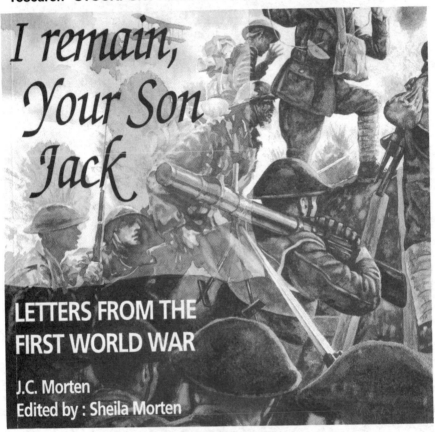

All of our books are available through your local bookseller. In case of difficulty, or for a free catalogue, please contact: **SIGMA LEISURE, 1 SOUTH OAK LANE, WILMSLOW, CHESHIRE S K9 6AR.**

Phone: 01625-531035; Fax: 01625-536800.
E-mail: sigma.press@zetnet.co.uk .
Web site: http://www.sigmapress.co.uk

VISA and MASTERCARD welcome. Please add £2 p&p to all orders.